KEVIN
SHEEDY

So Good I Did It Twice

KEVIN
SHEEDY
So Good I Did It Twice

WITH JOHN KEITH

Sport Media Ⓢ

This book is dedicated to my parents,
Jean and Michael, who supported,
encouraged, laughed and cried throughout
the highs and lows of my football career.
Also to my three beautiful children,
Mark, Lucy and Maria, who I love dearly
and am so proud of.

Kevin Sheedy

With grateful thanks to Everton FC official
statistician Gavin Buckland for supplying
career facts, figures and records from his
unrivalled bank of information.

Kevin Sheedy and John Keith

Sport Media

By Kevin Sheedy with John Keith

Copyright text: Kevin Sheedy and John Keith

Published in Great Britain in 2014.
Published and produced by: Trinity Mirror Sport Media,
PO Box 48, Old Hall Street, Liverpool L69 3EB.
Production: James Cleary
Design: Graeme Helliwell

Managing Director: Ken Rogers
Publishing Director: Steve Hanrahan
Executive Editor: Paul Dove
Executive Art Editor: Rick Cooke
Senior Marketing Executive: Claire Brown
Senior Book Sales Executive: Karen Cadman

Photographic acknowledgements:
Kevin Sheedy collection, Mirrorpix, PA Pics.
Front cover image: Tony Woolliscroft.

Printed and bound by CPI Group (UK) Ltd,
Croydon, CR0 4YY

Contents

About John Keith:

John Keith, who collaborated with Kevin on this book, has covered football as a journalist and broadcaster since the 1960s. He has written many books including biographies of Dixie Dean, Bill Shankly, Colin Harvey, Ian Callaghan and Billy Liddell.

John spent more than 30 years as a Daily Express staff sportswriter and is now Merseyside football correspondent for Ireland's national broadcasting service RTE.

After hosting BBC Radio Merseyside's Saturday Football Phone-In for a decade he now presents his own weekly chat show *Strictly John Keith* on City Talk 105.9.

He is also writer and presenter of *The Bill Shankly Story* and *The Dixie Dean Story* stage shows and his new production *Bob Paisley – Reluctant Genius* premieres at New Brighton Floral Pavilion in September 2014.

Foreword
By Howard Kendall

IF I hadn't been able to bring Neville Southall to Everton then Kevin Sheedy would rate as my best ever signing as a manager. I cannot offer praise higher than that.

Kevin's left foot was bewitching and while he is rightly remembered for the great goals he scored, his skills created so many more for his team-mates. In today's football parlance his assist statistics were sky high.

I was alerted to Kevin by my Goodison right hand man Colin Harvey. He'd seen Kevin play in Liverpool reserves but his career seemed to be going nowhere at Anfield. So Colin and I went to see him play in a Central League game at my old club Preston.

To be honest, Kevin just jogged through it. But that left foot of his was like a shining light! Colin felt we should take a chance and try to sign him. I thought about it and, being a great respecter of Colin's judgment, I decided we would.

But I said to Kevin: "As a midfield player you're going to have to work harder than that." He replied: "That was only the reserves...you'll have no worries on that score."

And, once we'd signed him, I never did. It was the best £100,000 of anyone's money. I realised Kevin wasn't going to make crunching tackles but his talent illuminated my Everton side.

Kevin made only five senior appearances in four seasons at Anfield, where Ronnie Whelan operated on the left of midfield, but he was a superb player for us during our unforgettable period in the 1980s. His total of 97 Everton goals in 369 appearances is phenomenal for a wide midfield player and it doesn't surprise me to learn that it's the most by a non-striker in the club's history.

Kevin's trademark, of course, were his spectacular

free-kicks...his twice-taken offering against Ipswich and his two scoring free-kicks at Charlton among them.

I liken his left foot to his fellow Ireland international Liam Brady's while former Liverpool manager Roy Evans said it was the best ever and Jamie Carragher declared that Kevin was the best free-kick taker he's ever seen, ahead of some famous names.

He was certainly a magician with a dead ball but I stress again his contribution to the team and to setting up goals for others was also superb. As a player he is, without doubt, an Everton great and he is now carving out a career in coaching.

It wouldn't surprise me if, one day, he moves into management. If so, I don't think he'd be one to use the 'hair dryer' treatment on his players. I think his style would be more diplomatic than that, using his ammunition wisely...just like he did delivering those devastating free-kicks.

What They Say

My Five Greatest Free-Kick Takers:

1. Kevin Sheedy
(Everyone was talking about dead ball specialists
since Leighton Baines' master class [last week].
But Sheedy was Everton's pioneer. I was
at the game in 1985 against Ipswich when he
entered folklore. After whipping one over the wall
and scoring, the referee spotted an infringement
and asked Sheedy to take it again. He did – and
promptly scored again, whipping the ball into
the opposite corner.

2. David Beckham
3. Ronald Koeman
4. Juninho
5. Sinisa Mihajlovic

*Jamie Carragher, Daily Mail,
September 27, 2013*

'The best left-footed player I ever played with'
Ireland legend Paul McGrath

1

Pub Football
How The Tram put me on the
right line to the top

MY football academy was situated between the A49
and the A465 just outside Hereford. It was there during my formative years that I developed the skills that
would eventually gain me a place in one of English
football's finest post-war teams and, arguably, the
greatest in the history of Everton Football Club.

But my own centre of excellence was unusual to say
the least, and a world away from the top-class facilities
that many of today's aspiring youngsters have at their
disposal.

Because my football learning curve began in a pub –
or, rather on three of its walls!

I was born in a pub at Builth Wells, Wales, in October 1959, but when I was four my mum and dad,
Michael and Jean, and my nan, Maria, bought a pub
called The Tram Inn Hotel, across the English border
at Allensmore, Herefordshire, where my older brother
Michael and I lived.

I quickly found a use for three of the pub walls. The
biggest one I used for shooting practice, hitting the
ball against it as hard as I could and controlling it as it
rebounded back. Another wall had a long window. It
was there that I'd practice my free-kicks and I'm glad
to say that only once did I break the glass.

The third wall included a gents' toilet, which was
three quarters the size of a goal. I used that to develop
my scoring art, which I'm sure helped me later in a
career that brought me more than 100 goals in senior
club football and nine for the Republic of Ireland, figures which, as a wide midfield player, I'm very proud
of.

As Everton's Academy coach the skills we aim to
instil into youngsters today are exactly the same as
the ones I acquired self-taught at The Tram. I'm
sure many past players, who took up the game long

before modern facilities were even dreamed of, used their own initiative to practice in their particular environment. For instance, my collaborator on this book, John Keith, tells me that the legendary Dixie Dean, the greatest centre-forward English football has ever seen, helped develop his phenomenal shooting and heading by hitting a ball against a chapel wall in the north end of Birkenhead. So I'm in good company.

My mum and dad were very supportive in helping me up the football ladder. My mum used to drive me to Hereford two nights a week to practice at the boys' club there, then sit in the car for a couple of hours waiting for me.

Later, my dad drove the minibus to take me with the Under-14s lads' club team to play in the Forest of Dean League and we'd stop on the way home for crisps and lemonade. It was hardly today's approved dietary regime but great, nevertheless! My best mate, Russell Pritchard, would always come with us. He was great at taking free-kicks – perhaps he had a good influence on me in that respect?

My dad's from Ennis, County Clare in Ireland, and used to play Gaelic football before coming to Britain at the age of 16. The hours my parents put in ensuring I could play football paid off. The lads' club coaches were Bob Dixon and Dewi Jones and Bob, who was a scout for Hereford United, invited me to train there twice a week.

We used to play under the Edgar Street lights on the shale car park on Tuesday and Thursday evenings. I was 15 and the manager, John Sillett, told me to ask Ken Lapsley, my headmaster at St Mary's, Lugwardine, if I could train every morning at Hereford and get the bus to school in the afternoon.

St Mary's was a rugby-playing school until my last couple of years there and missing classes every morning to play football would be unheard of today. But Mr Lapsley gave me permission. He probably realised that football was the career I'd set my heart on and kindly let me off to train daily with Hereford, which I'm sure benefited my development greatly.

The only condition he set was that if I ever played in a cup final he'd expect two complimentary tickets! So I was delighted a decade later to be able to send him a couple of tickets for the 1984 Milk Cup Final, the first all-Mersey Wembley occasion. He was overjoyed and it was a nice way to say thank you to him.

Hereford were then in the old Division Three, having been elected to the Football League only a couple of years earlier before winning promotion as

Division Four runners-up in their first season of 1972/73. When I was 16, Hereford kept their promise by signing me as an apprentice. Having played in goal as a boy in scratch six-a-side games at fetes and fairs my dad used to take me to, and then switching to striker, by the time I graduated to Hereford reserves I settled into a left centre-midfield role.

The reserves played in an open-age league, something many of today's youngsters are not exposed to. You could find yourself – sometimes quite painfully – facing streetwise seasoned pros and it was a great education for me.

I learned to look after myself on the field while off it, I was one of seven apprentices who had to do all the menial tasks such as cleaning boots, cleaning the dressing rooms, sweeping the stands after matches and painting parts of the ground. It was character building.

My specific daily job was to look after the referee's room where John Sillett, his assistant, Terry Paine, the famous former England and Southampton winger, and our reserve and youth-team coach, Tony Ford, got changed. I had to look after their kit and lay it out, as well as making sure their bath was at the right temperature.

One day I was in the first team dressing room, enjoying listening to the chat and the banter between our senior pros, when John, who was a larger than life character but disliked by some players because of his aggression, shouted: "Sheedy! Get your arse in here."

When I went in the three of them, Sillett, Paine and Ford, were standing naked in the bath amidst a collection of broken glass because somebody had gone in and deliberately smashed milk bottles in it. I had the job of clearing up the mess and I never found out who was the guilty party. If you did it and happen to be reading this, please let me know!

On another occasion Sillett suddenly appeared from his manager's office with a double-barrel shotgun – for which I presume he had a licence – took aim at a pigeon on the newly re-seeded pitch but managed only to wing it. He then gave me a stick and said to me: "Here son, you go and finish it off." So I had to put the poor creature out of its misery.

I was an apprentice for a year before I signed full professional forms on my 17th birthday in October 1976. I asked Sillett for a rise on my weekly wage of £28 and he increased it to £35.

But before he agreed, he said: "Are you going to try any harder?"

I replied: "Well, I can't try any harder than I have been doing." He just laughed and gave me my extra seven quid a week.

I have to say that John Sillett was great for me. He recognised my ability as a youngster, showed his faith in me and nurtured me along the football path. Terry Paine, too, passed on to me some valuable advice from his wealth of experience which had been honed from more than 800 league appearances for Southampton and Hereford, and inclusion in Sir Alf Ramsey's victorious 1966 England World Cup squad.

One of our players got sent off in a youth game against Torquay United for lashing out and punching one of their players after a high tackle. The next day in training Terry called him over and told him never again to get sent off for raising his arms. And Terry promptly demonstrated to him the dark art of going over the top of the ball. In those days especially, with tackling from behind allowed, wingers had to know how to look after themselves. Terry could certainly do that.

I made my senior debut in great circumstances in the final game of the 1975/76 season, at home to Preston, just after we'd won the old Third Division title. It was an evening match, I had total faith in my ability and it was exciting to run out as a first-team player. It was a landmark moment for me in my career.

I wore the No. 8 jersey and although we were 1-0 down at half-time that great goalscorer, Dixie McNeil, later to star for Wrexham, banged in a second half hat-trick to see us win 3-1 and finish on a high.

I'll never forget the atmosphere after the game, with the Third Division championship trophy having pride of place in our dressing room. The sight of that silverware spurred me on. It whetted my appetite for more.

Incidentally, Dixie's hat-trick that night took his league goals total that season to 34. His first name was Richard but the way he rattled the net certainly justified his nickname.

He also took me under his wing and made me feel a part of things, getting me involved in the card schools on the team bus. Whether that was wise or not I don't know...

Another man who played in that game, in the Preston No. 6 jersey, was a certain Mark Lawrenson. He was on his way to stardom at Liverpool, where we played together a few times and he eventually became a Republic of Ireland international teammate of mine.

Dixie McNeil scored a further 16 league goals in the

old Second Division in 1976/77 but as we were a team without much financial clout and punching above our weight, his output wasn't enough to prevent us finishing bottom to send us back into Division Three.

2

Bobby's Job

Face to face with the legends
who inspired me

MY career ignited on Merseyside but the flame was
lit in Manchester...or, more specifically, by two of Old
Trafford's finest: George Best and Bobby Charlton.
They were my boyhood heroes and the images of
those two wonderful players in action were imprinted
in my thoughts every time I went out to kick a ball
against the walls of our family's pub near Hereford.

George was fantastic, the definition of a fantasy
player. Many professionals, pundits and members
of the public tend to hail Pele or Maradona as the

greatest of all time and for me it was Maradona. I know that for England his name will forever revive dark memories of his 'Hand Of God' goal for Argentina in the 1986 World Cup quarter-final in Mexico. But his second goal of that game, when he ran and ran past bewildered England players Glenn Hoddle, Peter Reid, Kenny Sansom, Terry Butcher and Terry Fenwick before guiding the ball past Peter Shilton, was voted the greatest ever scored at a World Cup Finals.

And that's how I will always remember Diego Maradona, who led his country to ultimate triumph in 1986 and was named player of the tournament. He was a deadly pocket battleship of a player and his ammunition was sheer brilliance. Maradona appeared in 21 consecutive World Cup Finals matches spanning four tournaments between 1982 and 1994, while at club level he led Napoli to their first ever Serie A title in 1987 – adding the Italian Cup in the same season – and after winning the UEFA Cup in 1989, landed a second Italian title in 1990. He was a fantastic player brimming with skill.

However, with all due respect to Northern Ireland, if George Best had appeared for a leading football nation with the high profile of major tournament finals, I'm quite certain he would have been acclaimed during his era as the finest player in the world, which is what he was to me.

He could do everything: score goals, dribble, run with the ball in a way that mesmerised defenders and bewitched spectators; shoot, head and tackle. He was Roy of the Rovers and as hard as nails. No wonder Bill Shankly said that George would also have made a terrific full-back!

Although George played before the massive explosion in televised football, thank goodness we still have enough film of him in action to capture the dazzling breadth of his talent. One of my favourite moments is an incident in a Manchester United game against Chelsea when George was confronted by the fierce attentions of Ron 'Chopper' Harris. Ron came in with fearsome intent to 'do' George. But he just rode the challenge, went around the goalkeeper and guided the ball into the net for one of the 179 goals he scored for United in 467 appearances, which is a tremendous tally for a wide player.

George was Britain's first pop footballer, nicknamed 'The Fifth Beatle' with a celebrity column in the Daily Express. His excesses with women and booze ensured that his picture was as frequently used on newspaper front pages as it was on the back. His United career ended at the age of 28 in 1974. But he'd played for them, mostly magically, for 11 seasons. Sadly, his alcoholism took him to an early death at the age of 59 in 2005 but I don't agree with those people who, during his playing pomp, wanted to change and reform him.

During his playing days stories emanated from Old Trafford about team-mates physically trying to teach him a lesson. But I suspect that many critics of George's lifestyle were just envious that he did what he did off the field – then proceeded to produce brilliance on it.

My view is that George was George and that if you'd ever succeeded in changing any part of him you would probably have interfered negatively with his massive talent.

There is the famous story of George, having won a packet of money gambling, going back to his hotel room with Miss World and ordering champagne. When the waiter arrived with the bubbly he saw the room awash with cash and George's glamorous companion lying on the bed. "Tell me, Mr Best," asked the waiter, "where did it all go wrong?"

That may be true or may be myth but I prefer a different question – where did it all go right? Although George left us far too early he enjoyed life to the full and bequeathed a footballing legacy second to none. He was mesmerising. I'm just glad to be able to say that I played on the same pitch as George when he was with Fulham in September 1976 and I went on as a Hereford sub at Craven Cottage.

I sat out Hereford's opening games in the Second Division but made my entrance as a substitute in the seventh match. At that time Fulham were feted by the media. They were a celebrity club. The great Bobby Moore, who'd led England to World Cup glory in 1966, the hugely talented Rodney Marsh and George were in their team.

Only one substitute was allowed in those days and I went on to replace Steve Davey, Dixie McNeil's attacking partner, who had sustained what was later diagnosed as a fractured cheekbone from a flying elbow. John Sillett told me to take off my tracksuit and sent me on in his place. I didn't have any time to think about it and, to be honest, while I was on the bench I had been distracted by the sight of George's wife, Angie Best, sitting alongside us. She was a stunning-looking woman and I can remember watching her as much as the game.

Bobby Charlton also had a major influence on me. Whenever I played as a boy, *I WAS* Bobby Charlton.

I've since met him, once, at a dinner and I told him that he was an inspiration to me. Typical of him, he reacted very modestly. But there was nothing modest about the way he played the game.

Along with George and Denis Law he formed a fabulous United trio. The way Bobby scored goals with his ferocious shooting was superb. And the ball was always rising as it hit the net! Indeed, I tried to model myself on Bobby because of his scoring record from midfield: 249 goals in 754 United appearances.

He had superb technique and when I think of him in action I still see him rocketing the ball into the net from distance, with a bewildered goalkeeper wondering where it came from!

As for the other legendary Bobby – Bobby Moore – the first thing I did when I got on the same pitch as him in that game against Fulham was to foul him! It was a challenge that was the product of youthful enthusiasm and lack of respect. Bobby, realising the situation, just smiled.

To use a modern cliché, Fulham were on fire that day and beat us 4-1, with Marsh scoring a couple. After two more substitute appearances, I had to wait until the following March to make my second start for Hereford – a 2-1 home win over Sheffield United.

Bobby's Job

I scored my first goal for them in a 3-1 home win over Millwall in April, although I have to admit I don't remember anything about it, and ended that relegation season having made 16 league appearances wearing a variety of shirt numbers: 6, 7, 8, 9, 11 and 12.

It was sad for the club to go straight back down but I had secured a regular place and there were already reports of interest from other clubs including Bristol City and Wolves. But little more than a year later, the European champions beckoned. I was heading to Liverpool.

3

This Is Anfield
When a Liverpool welcome
wasn't a real Philip...

I SUPPOSE it was an omen about what lay in store for me when the most successful football manager of the 20th century shook hands with me and said after I'd signed for Liverpool: "Congratulations and good luck, Philip."

Those were the words of the great Bob Paisley as I sat in his windowless Anfield office, having putting pen to paper on a four-year contract to complete my £80,000 transfer from Hereford in July 1978. I was 18 years old.

I reminded Bob politely that my name was Kevin, but when I look back perhaps it was a sign of the way things would pan out for me at Anfield. To be honest, I didn't really want to go to Liverpool in the first place and one of the reasons I did sign was because Hereford did a bit of a con job on me.

Although Hereford had suffered a second successive relegation to the old Fourth Division, after finishing next to bottom of the Third the previous season, I had established myself in the team to the extent that I made 39 league and cup appearances that year, and weighed in with four goals. There was also increased newspaper speculation about other clubs being interested in me, which gave me great encouragement.

One day I got a telephone call from Dewi Jones, a coach and a friend of mine, offering me two Wembley tickets for the European Cup final between Liverpool and Bruges. I took him up on the offer, saw Kenny Dalglish score the winning goal and was also impressed by what I believed was the best midfield in Europe: Jimmy Case, Terry McDermott, Graeme Souness and Ray Kennedy.

A few weeks later I got a phone call at my family's pub from the Hereford chairman, Peter Hill, saying that they'd agreed a fee with Liverpool and they wanted me to travel to Merseyside to sign for them. It was all a bit of a rush but as my mum, dad and I were about to set off to drive to Anfield, my mum announced that she needed a new suit for the occasion. So we made a dash to Marks & Spencer and my dad and I sat in the car outside the store while my mum went in to choose a new outfit before we could leave!

In those days there weren't many agents around and I certainly didn't have one. If you needed advice or assistance you could go to the PFA, the Professional Footballers' Association.

But I remember thinking on the way up to Liverpool that I didn't want to sign for them. I'd just seen them beat Bruges, they were the best team in Europe and they had a track record of bringing in young players and keeping them in the reserves, with the aim of eventually bringing them through. My aim was for first-team football but what chance would I have? And with reports of other clubs being interested in me I was dead set against joining Liverpool.

When I arrived at Anfield I met Bob Paisley and it was all very impressive. They showed me around and my dad had his picture taken with the newly retained European Cup. We then discussed terms but for me it was never about money – it was about doing what was best for my career. Peter Hill was also present and he realised that I wasn't too keen on signing. So he called me to one side and said that Hereford needed the money and were in danger of going out of business. Then he promised that if I signed, Hereford would buy me a car.

Given the fact that Hereford had given me my chance, that I was a young hometown boy and also the threat to their survival as told to me by the chairman, I eventually put pen to paper. It was then that Bob congratulated me...and got my name wrong.

When the business had been concluded Peter Hill told my mum, dad and I to follow him and he'd show us the best route out of the city. I remember stopping at a newsagents and buying a *Liverpool Echo*, which carried a back page picture of me signing for Liverpool.

Three or four days later I rang Peter to ask about the car he'd promised me. He told me to get in touch with the Hereford club secretary, Bill Stevens, which I did. Bill led me out of his office, past a row of cars to a sky blue Cortina which was not only the rustiest vehicle you've ever seen but it wasn't even roadworthy. It wasn't first, second or third hand – more like fourth or fifth! It was horrendous and I told them they could stick their car, or words to that effect. I'd been well and truly stitched up, big time. It was my introduction to the real world and I look back on it now and laugh. But I have fond memories of Hereford and the start they gave me in football.

Liverpool had come in for me on the recommendation of their celebrated chief scout, Geoff Twentyman, but I never knew he was watching me because he would go to a game and pay at the turnstiles. He also assessed you more in away games than home matches.

But my career never took off at Liverpool because their recognised first team was well nigh invincible and they never seemed to get any injuries, mainly because of the way they played. They just overpowered opponents, rarely having to make last-ditch tackles or expose themselves to injury. It was as close to risk-free football as you could get.

I had the thankless task of vying for Ray Kennedy's role on the left of midfield, one he'd been switched to by Bob Paisley after playing as a striker in Arsenal's Double-winning side. I could also operate centrally. But there was no such thing as rotation in those days. They never rested anyone. If you were first choice and you were fit, you played.

To be honest, I tend to favour that selection policy

rather than the wholesale rotation some managers employ in the modern game. You see a centre-forward score a great goal, he's left out of the next game and when he's recalled he doesn't score for ages. He's lost the momentum.

I'm aware that the pace of the game has changed and that players are more accepting of rotation but, countering that, top-flight pitches today are almost unrecognisable from the stamina-sapping surfaces of yesteryear, tackling from behind has been banned and the balls are lighter. I fell out with every manager I played for if I wasn't in the team when I was fit. I always wanted to play, and I'm sure that applies just as much to players today.

When I joined Liverpool I shared digs with Alan Hansen in Elsie Road, Anfield, but when Alan eventually moved out I had a word with the landlady, Mrs Edwards, to ask if she would take in another young player I'd become pals with...Ronnie Whelan. Ronnie had arrived at Liverpool as an 18-year-old from Dublin club, Home Farm, and our respective career journeys from sharing those digs would take us all the way to playing together in the World Cup and European Championship for the Republic of Ireland.

My first season at Liverpool went quite well. Playing

for the reserves, we won the Central League under Roy Evans, something we did four times in my four years at Anfield. That team included goalkeeper Steve Ogrizovic, Howard Gayle and Sammy Lee. I remember Sammy, like many of us, feeling frustrated at the lack of first-team football and telling me on the bus going to training that he was a bit fed up. We all had to bide our time.

During my second season at Anfield I got a back injury, which proved something of a mystery. I had pain at the bottom of my back, and visits to the hospital and traction failed to cure it. Roy Evans and Ronnie Moran treated me at the club and because nobody knew what the problem was they had me down as being mentally weak. They'd leave me for ages just sitting on the bed waiting for treatment because they got it into their heads that the problem was psychological rather than physical.

Someone told me to try acupuncture. So, as a last resort I paid the fee to go to a practitioner in Liverpool's Rodney Street. And, whatever the problem was, that cured it – although I think by then a lot of damage had been done to my reputation within the club.

I had to wait until February 1981, more than two-

and-a-half years after moving from Hereford, before I got my first taste of the big time, making my debut in a 2-2 draw against Birmingham City in the old First Division at Anfield. Alan Hansen was ruled out and in a re-shuffle Ray Kennedy was switched to centre-back with me taking his place on the left of midfield.

Although I'd have liked to have been in a winning team – Birmingham came back from 2-0 down after David Johnson and Phil Neal had scored – I'm delighted to say that I was named as Liverpool's star man in the *Sunday People* the next morning. I hit a shot from 25 yards that rattled the bar at the Kop end. If that had gone in, who knows what would have happened? But I didn't manage to stay in the team.

A week later I found myself on the bench as an unused substitute in the 2-2 draw at Brighton & Hove Albion, which was the end of my association with the first team until the following autumn.

The following midweek after the Brighton game I got a great boost by being selected, along with Ronnie Whelan, in the Republic's Under-21 team against England at Anfield – but it was to prove a fateful game for my career. I remember taking a shot after the ball had broken to me outside the box at the Kop end and Mark Proctor of Middlesbrough, who'd come on as an England substitute, went over the top and did me. The result was an ankle injury that kept me out for almost a month.

I was still striving for full fitness after that setback when Ray Kennedy got injured and was ruled out of a Friday night game against Stoke. Ronnie Whelan was called in to replace him and had a brilliant debut, scoring the first goal in a 3-0 win and making a big impression. Ronnie took his opportunity when it was presented and went on eventually to replace Ray and have a fantastic Liverpool career. But it meant my chance had gone.

I ploughed on in the reserves with my parents watching me in every game, home and away, helping to keep my spirits up. But it was really difficult and, on reflection, I realised it toughened me mentally. Even when things didn't go so well later in my career I told myself that I could never feel so low as I did at that stage at Liverpool.

Yet my time at Anfield was invaluable in what I learned day to day in the five-a-side sessions in training. It was all pass and move, pass and move. It sounds simplistic but it's what football is.

The day after Bill Shankly's death stunned the nation, on September 29, 1981, I was named as a substitute for the second leg of the European Cup tie against Oulu Palloseura at Anfield. The sadness and emotion generated by the great man's passing was heavy in the Anfield air as I sat on the bench without getting on. But for someone who started the evening sitting alongside me it was to prove a landmark night.

Ian Rush replaced David Johnson in the 64th minute and four minutes later he scored the first of his club record 346 goals. Liverpool had lost an icon in Shanks, but a legend had been born in the shape of that lean and hungry Welshman, Rushie.

I stayed on the bench for the next two games – during which I managed just one minute on the pitch as a late, late replacement for David Johnson against Swansea – before the second leg of the League Cup tie at Exeter provided me with my second Liverpool start. I scored my first goal for the club in a 6-0 win that added up to an 11-0 aggregate victory. After two more stints as an unused substitute – against Sunderland and AZ Alkmaar – I started the next League Cup tie against Middlesbrough and opened the scoring in a 4-1 win, watched by little more than 16,000 Anfield spectators.

My last action in a Liverpool first-team shirt was in March as a substitute for Sammy Lee in a shock 1-0 home defeat by Brighton, with Alan Hansen conceding an own goal. Liverpool, though, marched on to the title, finishing with 87 points, four ahead of Ipswich and nine ahead of third-placed Manchester United.

After just three starts and two substitute appearances in four seasons at Anfield I knew I had to get away to re-ignite my career. One morning at Melwood, Ronnie Moran said that Bob Paisley wanted to speak to me. Bob informed me that Blackpool wanted to talk to me. But they were then in the old Fourth Division and I told them that I wasn't interested in the money offered – I wanted to play at a high level. I also believed that Derby County, then in the old Second Division, had made an offer for me which Liverpool had rejected.

Then, the night before the final reserve game of the season at Preston, I got a phone call from Colin Wood, the highly respected sportswriter of the *Daily Mail*. What he told me changed my life and transformed my career – and I didn't even have to pack my bags!

4

Howard's Call

Battling to prove my worth
on the other side of Stanley Park

WHEN the phone rang at my digs on the evening
of Friday, May 14, 1982, what transpired was – I
suspected – a wind-up, some kind of practical joke.
Britain was gripped by events thousands of miles away
in the Falklands War, the football season was about
to end and my career at Liverpool had been plunged
into a worrying limbo.

I knew I had little future at Liverpool, even though
they'd offered me a new four-year contract. They also
told me they were open to offers for me.

I was a regular in Liverpool's reserve side and was preparing for the next day's final Central League fixture at Preston North End when the phone rang.

I picked it up to be greeted by Colin Wood, who said to me: "Would you be interested in signing for Everton?"

Taken by surprise and, like I say, wary of a leg-pull, I replied: "I certainly would."

"Okay," said Colin. "If you put the phone down it will ring again shortly and it will be Howard Kendall on the line."

And, sure enough, the phone did ring almost immediately and it was Howard calling.

"I'm coming to watch you play tomorrow," he said. "Would you be interested in signing for Everton?"

"Of course I would, Mr Kendall," I replied, my thoughts racing with excitement.

"Okay – but there's just one thing," he added. "I've heard you don't try all the time. That's what I've been told."

"Mr Kendall," I replied, feeling a little bit riled by what he'd said. "I ALWAYS try. I can assure you of that."

Needless to say, I had even extra determination to perform well the following day, which I think I did.

Howard's Call

A week later, by which time I'd gone back home to Hereford, I got a call from Everton's chief scout, Harry Cooke, inviting me to Bellefield to meet Howard with a view to signing.

So I drove back up to Merseyside, still without an agent and negotiating the business myself. I had yet to meet Howard but with memories of feeling co-erced into signing for Liverpool almost four years earlier, I said to myself: 'This time just listen to what they've got to say, think about it, sleep on it and then make a decision'.

But Howard, who had a great relationship with the media, had set things up with the press for a photo-story of me signing for Everton and flying out with them the next day on an end-of-season 'bonding' trip to Thailand. He made me a wage offer and we talked about a signing-on fee.

I also said to him: "I would like a house."

He said: "We can't do that for you, son."

I'm told he laughingly called me a cheeky so-and-so and I never got the house – not even a two-up, two-down!

We did reach agreement, though, but he certainly wasn't happy when I told him that I wanted 24 hours to have a good think about it.

I learned later that because I hadn't put pen to paper that day, Howard decided not to sign me. The next day, by which time Everton had flown out to Thailand, I rang Harry Cooke to tell him I would be delighted to sign.

There were no mobile phones or e-mails in those days and when Harry contacted Howard he was sitting by the pool at the Thai hotel, quaffing champagne and still mulling over whether to sign me or not. I think the next glass or two must have mellowed him because Howard rang Harry back and told him to sign me.

So I travelled back up to Bellefield to sign the transfer forms and become an Everton player. The clubs, though, could not agree a fee. Everton offered £60,000 and Liverpool wanted £200,000, which was considerably more than the £80,000 they'd paid for me from Hereford. The logjam lasted for weeks that summer, and the matter was set to be heard by an independent tribunal. But costs and the unpredictable nature of tribunal decisions eventually persuaded the clubs to settle amicably on a fee of £100,000 just 24 hours before the scheduled hearing.

It was an exciting new start for me and I had joined a small group of players who have made the move across Stanley Park from Anfield to Goodison. I was the first to do so for 20 years, since Johnny Morrissey in 1962. Conveniently, I was in the same city but being aware of the blue and red rivalry I knew I had to make a positive, early impression. I didn't want Everton supporters asking: "If he's not good enough for Liverpool, why should he be good enough for us?"

During my time at Liverpool I used to go to Goodison to watch Everton's midweek matches and I enjoyed the atmosphere there. I could see young players coming in and I was impressed by the team Howard was building.

I remember vividly one of Graeme Sharp's early outings against Leeds United, when he battered Kenny Burns after the big centre-half had tried unsuccessfully to intimidate him early on, and crowned his display by scoring the only goal of the game. I also saw Adrian Heath – 'Inchy' – come into the Everton side after his £750,000 move from Stoke, and watched Kevin Ratcliffe launch his great career.

So I threw myself into pre-season training brimming with enthusiasm and determination, and I pulled on the No. 11 Everton jersey for the first time against Lokeren in a four-club tournament in Bruges. We lost 4-3 but won our second game against Genoa, 2-1. The fact that Adrian Heath and Graeme Sharp scored four of our five goals in those two games was a positive sign of things to come.

I made my senior debut for Everton at promoted Watford in the old First Division on Saturday, August 28, 1982, and the team – in shirt number order was: Neville Southall, Brian Borrows, John Bailey, Mark Higgins, Billy Wright, Heath, Steve McMahon, David Johnson, Sharp, Andy King and me.

Kevin Richardson was on the bench as the single substitute allowed at that time. He replaced McMahon but we went down 2-0 to a Watford side managed by Graham Taylor and with John Barnes and Luther Blissett supplying ammunition for lanky striker Ross Jenkins.

Obviously it wasn't the start that we'd hoped for, although many other teams were to come unstuck against Watford's direct, long-ball style, which would drive them to runners-up spot behind Liverpool that season, in which we finished seventh.

On the team coach coming back from Watford I remember Howard saying our season started from then and we responded by hammering European champions Aston Villa 5-0 on my home debut at Goodison the following Tuesday evening, with Heath and Sharp scoring two apiece and King weighing in with the other. I knew it was a big game for me and I put myself under a lot of pressure in the build-up.

As I reached the top of the steps from the players' tunnel onto the pitch I knew I was stepping out in front of fans who'd be examining my every move and analysing the performance of the player who'd 'crossed the park'. But I played well and it was a superb team display which put us 3-0 up at half-time. It felt even better on the Saturday when we were home again, to Tottenham.

I scored my first Everton goal after only seven minutes, which gave me a wonderful feeling – and to do it against former Liverpool goalkeeper, Ray Clemence, who I'd known from my Anfield days, made it even sweeter. My shot flew past Ray and it obviously made a big impression on broadcaster, Billy Butler, a fervent Everton fan. Billy wrote in his *Liverpool Echo* column: 'The first time Ray Clemence saw Kevin Sheedy's shot was on *Match of the Day* on Saturday night!'

As I sat in the dressing room after the game I felt a sense of intense pleasure – and some relief. I was really pleased because I felt that I'd managed to remove any reservations some of the Everton supporters might have had about my move from Liverpool. Howard was delighted, too. He knew that I was a player who really did try!

In the league our results were up and down until we hit April, when we went on a run of six wins, a draw and only one defeat in our final eight games. In the FA Cup we went down to the only goal of the quarter-final at Manchester United, my Republic of Ireland colleague Frank Stapleton breaking our hearts by scoring a minute from the end.

Right at the start of the FA Cup trail that season I popped in a crucial late goal when we were losing 1-0 to Newport County, then in the old Third Division. They'd already done well against us in the League Cup the previous October before we went through on a 4-2 aggregate.

But we were trailing 1-0 at their Somerton Park ground with only three minutes of the third-round tie remaining when I managed to grab an equaliser and spare us the embarrassment of one of the worst results in Everton history.

At the end of the 1982/83 season I was just glad that I'd established myself in the Everton team, playing in 48 of the club's 51 games, and scoring 13 goals.

My career had been transformed – but Howard

Howard's Call

Kendall and Everton would have to weather severe storms before we'd experience shining success and bask in the glitter of silverware.

5

Winter Blues
How Howard weathered the storm and laid the path to glory

I DOUBT if there's ever been a season of starker contrast in Everton history than the 1983/84 campaign, ranging from abject gloom and record low attendances to Wembley glory and silverware on the sideboard. And I think, amidst the turmoil and roller coaster fortunes that season produced, that it was a lesson in the finer arts of management demonstrated by Howard Kendall.

During that so-called 'winter of discontent' at Goodison I think Howard's superb relationship with the media bought himself some time. I think the press didn't sink their teeth into him as they could have done, given our poor results during that grim period. Just after Christmas in 1983 we lost 3-0 at rock-bottom Wolves, leaving us 16th in the old 22-club First Division. We'd scored only five league goals at Goodison and six away from home, and we were only five points above the relegation zone.

The supporters, quite understandably, did not like what they were seeing and voted with their feet. The attendance for our third round League Cup tie against fellow First Division side Coventry City in November, for example, was a mere 9,080, the lowest recorded at Goodison for a competitive match between top-flight clubs.

It was not a pleasant situation for the players, but imagine what it must have been like for Howard. The buck stops with the manager and he was under great pressure, even to the point of arriving home after one game to be greeted with sympathy by his wife after she'd heard a shockingly erroneous BBC radio report that he'd been sacked, and Mike England appointed in his place!

Yet, through it all, Howard kept the lines of communication with the press wide open.

Winter Blues

That is a pre-requisite for a manager, especially today with rolling 24/7 news outlets. But even then, prior to the arrival of digital television and the internet, it was essential for a manager to have a good relationship with the media. And it's a two-way street. There might be something on a particular day that the manager feels, for the benefit of the club, he'd rather not disclose or talk about. In exchange he can trade another story to the news gatherers and so both parties end up satisfied. From what I'm told, Bill Shankly was a master in his dealings with the press, quite apart from all his other qualities. In my experience there's been nobody better than Howard.

I'm sure that during that winter of 1983 his press relations were a critical factor in ensuring he came through that turbulent period, during which leaflets were distributed by some fans calling for Howard to be sacked. What a great decision by club chairman Philip Carter (later Sir Philip) to accept John Keith's invitation to write a signed article in the *Daily Express* confirming his faith and confidence in Howard as Everton manager.

At the end of that season my team-mates were running around Wembley with the FA Cup after beating Watford to climax a run of only five defeats in 36 games since that Christmas crash at Molineux. Unfortunately, I missed the last 14 games of the season, including the FA Cup Final, thanks to a tackle by Liverpool's Phil Neal in the League Cup Final (then under the Milk Cup banner) at Wembley, the first all-Merseyside meeting at the famous old stadium. It wasn't a nice challenge and I felt, rightly or wrongly, that it wasn't accidental.

I broke through the Liverpool defence, with Neal the last defender and his challenge ruptured my ankle ligaments and finished my season prematurely. The game finished goalless and I underwent ankle surgery the following midweek on the day of the replay at Maine Road, which we lost through Graeme Souness's only goal of the game.

Three games before the Wembley final, my run of 76 consecutive appearances, stretching back to November 1982, ended when I was injured in our 2-1 FA Cup quarter-final win at Notts County, by which time I'd scored 10 goals. I told Howard before the Notts County game that I was having fitness problems twisting and turning. He told me he was still going to play me, but added: "Just run in straight lines!"

That's what I did, and I delivered the free-kick for Andy Gray to score with a spectacular diving header to give us the victory. After missing the next three games I was fit to return against Liverpool, only to fall victim to that Phil Neal tackle which cost me a place in the FA Cup Final, the worst feeling any player can have.

My misfortune meant opportunity for Kevin Richardson, who came in for the remaining games. The team's recovery after the turn of the year, culminating in the FA Cup win and a seventh-place finish in the league, was down to Howard's management and team-building ability. His signing of Peter Reid for £60,000 from Bolton and his much-questioned acquisition of injury-haunted Andy Gray for £250,000 from Wolves, allied to the promotion of Colin Harvey to work alongside Mick Heaton as first-team coach, were inspired decisions.

Of all the managers I played for – and they include Bob Paisley, Kevin Keegan and Jack Charlton – without doubt Howard was the best. The way he battled through that 1983 so-called winter of discontent to lead us to the FA Cup followed by two league titles, the Cup Winners' Cup and runners-up in league and FA Cup in 1986 was the product of masterful leadership.

His man-management skills were fantastic, and not

just with the players in the team. Dealing with them is relatively easy. But Howard was great in the way he treated players who were not in the side, by making them feel part of the group and nurturing team spirit. He could also relax, another quality essential for a manager to possess. On the way home from away matches he'd often ask the coach driver to stop at an off-licence and get a crate of beer on board. He saw it as part of team-bonding.

I remember after we'd had a good away win at QPR I was presented with a jeroboam of champagne after being named Man of the Match. On the bus home I asked Howard for a glass to have a drop of the bubbly and before I knew it there was champers all round for the rest of the lads up and down the bus.

Howard always managed with a laid-back, light touch approach unlike Colin Harvey, after he'd been promoted when Howard left for Athletic Bilbao in 1987. Colin just couldn't seem to relax. It was always high pressure in training every day. He was intense all the time. It was the way he was. I also felt that Colin went down the slippery slope of replacing great players with good ones – Stuart McCall for Peter Reid, Pat Nevin for Trevor Steven, Neil McDonald for Gary Stevens are examples of what I mean.

Winter Blues

Howard as a manager would delegate much of the training to Colin and Mick Heaton, and join in our five-a-sides himself. But when Colin became manager he didn't seem able to do that. He couldn't let go. There was a similar situation when I was at Blackburn Rovers as youth coach. Kenny Dalglish moved upstairs to become the club's director of football after managing Blackburn to the Premier League title in 1995. Ray Harford was promoted from coach – and a very good one he was – to succeed Kenny as manager. He was taking charge of the reigning champions but Ray found it hugely problematical.

As a coach his remit was just to deal with football matters in training and on the pitch. But as a manager you have a host of other responsibilities, not least dealing with the media, and it takes a certain type of person to be able to do that, especially today with such concentrated media focus and foreign players to deal with.

6

World Class

"If they'd worn yellow, blue and green
we'd have called them Brazil!"

I WAS fortunate to play in many wonderful matches
in my career, but the one that dominates my memory
was staged at Goodison Park on Saturday, October
27, 1984 – the day I fully realised that I was part of an
Everton team that was heading for the stars. Manchester United, on the same 20-point total as us but ahead
on goal difference in third place behind pace-setters
Arsenal and Sheffield Wednesday, were the visitors.

Ron Atkinson's side had lost only once up to that
stage and were favourites for the league title. But the

goal difference between the sides on that afternoon was massively in our favour – 5-0 to be precise. Our line-up, in a 4-4-2 formation, was:

Neville Southall; Gary Stevens, Derek Mountfield, Kevin Ratcliffe, Pat Van Den Hauwe; Trevor Steven, Peter Reid, Paul Bracewell and myself; Adrian Heath, Graeme Sharp. Substitute: Andy Gray.

United also paraded a 4-4-2 formation:

Gary Bailey; Kevin Moran, Gordon McQueen, Graeme Hogg, Arthur Albiston; Remi Moses, Gordon Strachan, Bryan Robson, Jesper Olsen; Mark Hughes, Alan Brazil. Substitute: Frank Stapleton.

Earlier that season, after United had put five goals past Newcastle and then West Ham at Old Trafford, one national newspaper ran the back page headline: 'Give Them The Title Now!' But the pundits and bookies who fancied United for the championship were forced into a swift re-assessment after we'd finished with them. We didn't just beat United: we attacked incessantly and demolished them.

I'd missed the previous six league and cup games with an ankle problem and my place had been taken in one match by Terry Curran, in two games by Kevin Richardson and in three by Alan Harper. But, thankfully, I was fit to return to face United and I didn't let the Goodison grass grow under my feet because with only five minutes gone I scored what, for me, was a very unusual goal – a header. Gary Stevens crossed the ball and I was about 18 to 20 yards out, wondering what I should do. So I positioned myself to head the ball, something I wasn't noted for. The next thing I knew, the ball flew past Gary Bailey into the top corner of the Park End net and I was lying on the turf feeling a bit stunned and not knowing quite what had happened except that I'd scored!

I had to be taken off to have four stitches in a head wound and it was only afterwards that I learned that, from the same incident, United defender and my Ireland colleague and friend, Kevin Moran, had been stretchered off and taken to hospital, to be replaced by another Ireland team-mate, Frank Stapleton.

The goal set us off towards a superb win. I scored again with a powerful shot to put us 2-0 up after 24 minutes. The move started in the left-back position and was continued by Adrian Heath, who slipped me in after I'd overlapped. There were further goals from Adrian, Gary Stevens and Graeme Sharp. It was a brilliant performance and a wonderful exhibition of total football.

But I didn't know the real story of my first goal until

the full action replay was relayed to me by Kevin Moran many years later. Kevin rang me to arrange a game of golf at Hillside, Southport. Over a drink after our round we were talking football and Kevin asked me what was the best goal I'd ever scored.

"It was when I rose above you and bulleted that header into the top corner," I told him. Kevin, who was always known as a hard, committed player, replied: "Do you want to know what really happened?" And he proceeded to tell me. "When the ball came across, your head was in the way of it and I ended up head-butting the back of your head and the ball flew in."

There had been nothing premeditated on Kevin's part. He was just trying to attack the ball. But I had no idea what had happened until that day long after at the 19th hole. I suppose you could say the goal was a double-header!

Our win, and the quality of the opposition we had demolished, made everyone sit up; public, press and pundits alike.

I was told later that one of the greatest accolades came from a supporter savouring his after-match pint in the Winslow pub, across the road from Goodison. "If that Everton team had been wearing yellow, blue and green we'd have called them Brazil," he declared, as he supped his beer. Our season, though, went from beer to champagne.

Three days after beating United at Goodison the lads – minus yours truly because of a groin injury – went to Old Trafford and knocked United out of the Milk Cup before I returned the following Saturday and weighed in with a goal in a 3-0 home win over Leicester City, which put us top of the league for the first time since February 1979.

Apart from a fortnight at the turn of the year that's where we stayed through to the end, clinching the title with five games to spare.

Starting with our FA Charity Shield win over Liverpool at Wembley, followed by the league title, our Cup Winners' Cup triumph and run to the FA Cup Final it was the greatest season in Everton's long history, spanning 63 games in five competitions. But it was the sheer quality and football exuberance of that autumn win over United that told us just what we could achieve.

7

Double Trouble
The day that lightning
DID strike twice

I'VE always enjoyed taking free-kicks. It was a speci-
ality of mine, part of my armoury with which I could
inflict big damage on the opposition. But none of the
ones I've taken can really compare with what happened at Goodison in March 1985.

The occasion – one that had a tragic conclusion
– was the FA Cup quarter-final tie against Ipswich
Town. We were only six minutes into the game when
we were awarded a free-kick in an inviting position
about a yard outside the box.

Kevin Sheedy

Throughout my playing career I always believed in taking free-kicks as quickly as possible, to capitalise on any advantage if the goalkeeper wasn't quite ready or well positioned. So, sticking to that policy, I got to the ball really early and with the Ipswich wall not set up properly, I bent it over them and into the top right-hand corner of goalkeeper Paul Cooper's net.

Goodison exploded in celebration. But our delight was swiftly extinguished when referee, Alan Robinson, disallowed it on the basis that I'd taken it before he'd signalled, and he ordered the kick to be re-taken.

Now it was a little bit of a mind game between me and the keeper. I could see Paul edging over towards the side I'd put the original kick, obviously feeling I was going to do the same again. But in doing so he left a little bit of a gap to his left.

At this point there was an intervention from my friend and team-mate, Peter Reid, who came over to me and said: "What are WE going to do now?" This coming from a man who scored a goal every Preston Guild! Actually, in fairness to Peter he managed 13 in 235 Everton appearances. That said, Peter was a great player but not when I had the ball at my feet waiting to re-take a free-kick. So I said to him: "Just get out of the fucking way, I'll stick it in the other corner."

Double Trouble

Although the Ipswich wall was better organised second time around, I managed to dink the ball over them and into the opposite, left side of the net. This time it DID count and my double-take made the feeling all the sweeter. Goodison erupted, providing me with one of the greatest moments of my Everton career. It must have been special for the fans, too, because they always mention it to me. It's as if it's stored by supporters in a collective memory bank.

Ipswich, though, gave us a big fright by coming back and taking the lead. They were still in front with five minutes left. But Derek Mountfield, that remarkable goalscoring centre-back, rescued us with an equaliser and we went on to win the replay and go all the way to Wembley.

Shortly after the final whistle at Goodison we were told the tragic news that former Everton manager, Harry Catterick, who'd watched the game, had collapsed and died. By poignant coincidence, Tommy Eggleston, who'd been at Harry's side at Everton during his highly successful period in charge between 1961 and 1973 and was briefly caretaker-manager, was also at Goodison. Tommy was there as Ipswich physio but, sadly, never reached Harry before he died.

The other tragic coincidence was that Harry, who'd

played for Everton as a centre-forward in the 1940s and '50s and scored 24 goals in 71 appearances, died in the same stand in which the legendary Dixie Dean had passed away watching a Merseyside derby five years earlier.

I never had the pleasure of meeting Harry but two league titles and two FA Cup Finals – one winning, one losing – plus remarkable league consistency show why he was noted as Everton's most successful manager until Howard Kendall took charge.

Two seasons after my twice-taken free-kick against Ipswich I had another free-kick double, but this time totally separate, one in each half, at Charlton in October 1986 – and both counted. I put the free-kicks in different sides of the net after I'd seen their keeper, Nicky Johns, do what Paul Cooper did, by starting to edge to either the left or right. They both went in but the gloss was taken away because we lost the game 3-2.

One of my free-kicks that was of huge significance came on a day when I produced one of my poorest performances in an Everton shirt. It was the FA Cup semi-final against Luton Town at Villa Park in April 1985. I had failed a late fitness test and missed our previous game, a goalless draw at Bayern Munich in the first leg of the European Cup Winners' Cup semi-final. Kevin Richardson had come in and done a really good job, playing his part in a great result.

On the Saturday morning of the FA Cup semi I was passed fit, and it was down to Howard Kendall whether he brought me back in or stuck with the team that had done so well in West Germany. In the event he gave me a massive confidence boost by picking me and naming Alan Harper as our one permitted substitute. So poor Kevin didn't even make the bench after his impressive contribution in Munich!

When Kevin saw me play that day he might have wondered why. Nothing I tried seemed to come off and after going behind to Ricky Hill's first-half goal it looked as if we were heading out. But to Howard's credit, he kept me on the pitch and four minutes from the end we won a free-kick, which gave me my chance to make an impact.

It wasn't one of the best I've ever struck but I spotted a gap at the side of the Luton wall and managed to squeeze the ball into the space and past goalkeeper Les Sealey. The ball certainly didn't fly in. It bobbled and just went over Les's hand and into the net. But it was a crucial goal and got us out of jail because on the day a very good Luton team, which included Mick

Harford and Brian Stein up front, had played well and they were tough to play against.

But that late goal worked wonders for us. We never lacked determination and our sheer will-to-win took us through in extra-time when Derek Mountfield – that man again – got on the end of my free-kick to take us to Wembley.

Probably the free-kick of mine that stirred most controversy – or rather the aftermath of it – came at Anfield in April 1987, at a time when Liverpool and ourselves were involved in a private Merseyside battle for the league title. We went into the game as league leaders, six points ahead of Kenny Dalglish's side, but they took a ninth-minute lead through Steve Mc-Mahon, a former Everton player scoring against his old club.

As a former Liverpool player I had the chance to do the same in reverse shortly after when we got a free-kick about 25 yards out at the Kop end, which prompted a buzz of anticipation from our fans. I think Liverpool supporters, too, knew what I was capable of doing and they were fearing the worst, from their point of view. I didn't disappoint them! It was the best free-kick I've ever hit and it soared past their goalkeeper, Mike Hooper, into the top corner of the net. To be honest, they could have had Ray Clemence and Bruce Grobbelaar in goal as well and they still wouldn't have stopped it!

I felt absolutely delighted to have scored with a strike like that and acting purely off the cuff in my moment of sheer joy I went to the Kop – where there were also Evertonians, by the way – and gave them a two-finger salute.

Adrian Heath came in behind me and made a similar gesture and, naturally, what we had done incensed Liverpool fans. Sad to say, we lost the game 3-1 through two further goals from Ian Rush, but the lasting pleasure was ours because we finished as champions, nine points ahead of Liverpool.

On the Monday after the derby, Adrian and I received notification from the FA, informing us we were to attend a disciplinary commission at their then Lancaster Gate headquarters in London to explain our actions at Anfield. As the FA had imposed £1,500 fines for similar gestures, that was the least we expected as Adrian and I travelled by train to the hearing with Everton secretary, Jim Greenwood.

We were also unsure as to whether the club could also face a fine. What we'd done had been shown and

re-shown on *Match of the Day* and other TV programmes, so the evidence was there at the flick of a
switch.

When we arrived we were ushered into a room in
front of two elderly FA representatives. They played
a VHS recording of my Anfield goal and subsequent
events, and asked us to explain our actions.

I said: "Well, I've just scored a goal at the Kop end..."
At that point they stopped the tape and, unbelievable
as it sounds, one of the FA men asked me: "How do
you know it was the Kop end?"

As you can imagine, Adrian and I just looked at each
other dumbfounded by that question. I went on to say:
"Well, it does look as if I've used two fingers but when
I score I raise one finger."

Adrian said something similar and then there was a
short adjournment. I had been sent off in a Milk Cup
tie at Chelsea 18 months earlier for "foul and abusive
language" but when the FA people returned they said
they had decided, in view of our previous good con-
duct, to take no action against either of us.

It was bizarre but we'd somehow got away with it
and we went back on the train unable to believe our
luck, but also well aware that the FA needed to get
their act together.

Double Trouble

My derby gesture at Anfield has since taken on a humorous life of its own because when I do after-dinner talks I use it in a Ted Rogers *3-2-1* routine, which always goes down well with the audience. Talk about the fickle finger of fate!

8

Glory Daze
"Your team played like a gang of Glasgow brothers"

GOODISON PARK has been the stage for so many special matches, many before my time, but I doubt if the famous old stadium has ever been as noisy as it was for the visit of Bayern Munich in April 1985 in the second leg of the European Cup Winners' Cup semi-final.

The barrage of sound got our adrenalin pumping, so goodness knows what it did to Bayern. An hour-and-a-half before kick-off the crowds were so big that our team coach couldn't get past the Park End of the ground. Right around the stadium was just thronged with people and you could sense that this was going to be no ordinary night.

Bayern's coach, Udo Lattek, said before the game that this match should have been the final and that whoever emerged victorious would win the cup. How right he was. But not in the way he hoped!

When we went out for the warm-up, even just reaching the top step onto the pitch, you could feel the electricity in the atmosphere. It just hit you as if it was something physical. I've never known anything like it. Playing in front of almost 50,000 fans, overwhelmingly ours, generating that kind of passion, we felt we just couldn't lose, even against opposition of Bayern's class and pedigree.

Like me, Andy Gray had missed the first leg in West Germany because of injury. Kevin Richardson and Alan Harper were drafted in and Trevor Steven told by Howard to support Graeme Sharp up front. Kevin cleared a shot off our line and Neville Southall made a fine save to deny Michael Rummenigge a goal which ensured the goalless draw that set up the second leg nicely.

In the fortnight before the Goodison return, we had beaten Luton Town 2-1 after extra-time in that FA

Cup semi-final at Villa Park. Then, we put four West Brom in the league at Goodison, when I was on target again.

I then managed to make it three goals in as many games when we went to Stoke City and won 2-0, sending us into the second leg collision with Bayern 10 points clear at the top of the league and on a run of 23 games unbeaten. Our confidence was sky high – we were ready for them!

But things didn't quite go according to plan because after 37 minutes Bayern scored in a breakaway from one of our corners. Lothar Matthaus sent Ludwig Kogl through on goal and although Neville stopped his initial shot, Dieter Hoeness, following up, scored from the rebound. Our fans were stunned. Suddenly, you could have heard a pin drop.

I was behind Neville on the goalline, trying to read what Hoeness would do. I think he might have mishit it. Whatever, it ended up in our net, the first goal we'd conceded in Europe that season. It also ended our British record sequence of seven consecutive European clean sheets, spanning 11 hours, seven minutes. Much more importantly, though, Bayern now had an away goal and our task had just become a whole lot harder.

They went in at half-time with their tails up but when we got to the dressing room Howard geed us up and lifted us. He reminded us that we were attacking the Gwladys Street end in the second half and told us the old adage: "Our fans will suck the ball into the net!" He also stressed the importance of keeping a high tempo and to get at Bayern, not allowing them a moment to dwell on the ball.

When we went out for the restart our fans had got over the shock of Bayern scoring and they made a terrific noise. It was just incredible. Riding on that vocal backing it took us only three minutes to level the scoreline.

The goal followed a long throw by Gary Stevens. It wasn't something we'd worked on but when the ball came in Andy Gray was in the box and flicked it on for Graeme Sharp to score at the far post. It was Sharpy's 29th goal of the season, extending his record of scoring in every European round that season, and it lit the blue touchpaper for us and clearly took Bayern out of their comfort zone.

Andy Gray wasn't giving them any comfort either and, in turn, he got a lot of stick. Eventually, his patience snapped and he kicked out at his marker, Hans Pfluger. Fortunately for Andy, and us, the Swedish referee, Eric Frederiksson, produced only a yellow card. Another Bayern defender, Norbert Eder, went off for treatment to a broken nose after another tussle with Andy.

With the break in play, Howard called me over – and our conversation was the subject of questions from the audience at a recent sportsman's dinner I attended when a video of the match showed me talking to Howard. People wanted to know if Howard was passing on some great tactical advice to me. Far from it. What Howard said was: "Tell that Scottish twat Sharpy to stop running offside!"

With the game now a rugged contest I later learned that Lattek shouted at our dug-out: "Kendall – this isn't football – this is war. You are all mad men." I'll let you guess what reply he got!

He was one to talk because his players dished it out, too. Peter Reid was done by the Danish midfielder, Soren Lerby. Reidy had stud mark holes in his shin that were so bad that our physio, John Clinkard, said they needed stitching. But Reidy just stuck a sponge down his blood-soaked sock and waded back into battle in typical style.

With 17 minutes left it was still 1-1 on the night and on aggregate, which meant Bayern's away goal would take them through. But with the fans still generating a wall of sound we scored our second – and the final was in sight. It was another long throw from Gary that set it up. Andy threw himself forward to connect with it, Bayern keeper Jean-Marie Pfaff fatally hesitated and Andy forced the ball into the net. For the first time in the tie we were in front.

The game then really opened up. We were attacking. They were attacking. But four minutes from the end we clinched our place in the club's first – and, so far, only – European final with a move I started when I took possession in the left-back position.

As I waited for Andy to make a run it seemed that 50,000 people were shouting to me "man on." I knew that. But I had to wait for Andy's move. When he made his run I played the ball in, Andy played it on to Trevor Steven and he went through and hit a great shot into the net.

The whole ground just erupted. It was like a volcano going off. And the celebrations continued in the dressing room. It had been a great display by us. We'd gone behind yet come back to see off the favourites for the trophy, not just with skill but every ounce of effort – and more – that we could summon up.

We were on the pitch taking the salute of the fans

following our 3-1 win which booked our place in the final and, in turn, applauding them for their fantastic support when I got a tap on the shoulder from one of the Bayern players.

He asked me if we could swap jerseys and was about to take his off and hand it over when I had to disappoint him. I told him I couldn't do an exchange because my shirt had to be washed for me to wear in the league game against Norwich City three days later!

I don't think he quite understood. Bayern players obviously had several sets of kit and were able to do swaps. Of course, it's very different today when shirt swapping is commonplace among players. That shows how much times have changed.

Plenty of nice things were written about us after the game but perhaps the greatest compliment on our victory came from Alex Ferguson, then Aberdeen manager, who'd watched the game then came to our dressing room afterwards to tell Howard and Colin Harvey: "You were magnificent tonight. Your team played like a band of Glasgow brothers." I doubt if there's higher praise than that.

As we approached the 1985 Cup Winners' Cup final against Rapid Vienna in Rotterdam, we had to recognise the lurking danger that could have come from within our own camp. There was perhaps a hidden threat to our ambition of adding Everton's name to the roll of honour of English clubs who have won European trophies. After seeing off strongly fancied Bayern, the mantle – and, maybe, the burden – of favourites was now draped around our shoulders and there was a risk of complacency setting in.

We would be facing Rapid as English champions and we also had the FA Cup Final against Manchester United looming at Wembley three days after the Rotterdam match.

So it was crucial we didn't take our eyes off the ball. But Howard made sure that by the time we flew out to Holland there was only one objective in our sights: to bring back that handsome – and now mothballed – European trophy.

And that's precisely what we did, without being overly extended. We performed well on the night, although at half-time it was still goalless after we'd had a couple of early chances. Andy Gray did put the ball in the net shortly before the interval but it was ruled offside.

After the interval, though, we turned our command of the game into goals. We went ahead when Graeme

Sharp intercepted a back pass, rounded the Rapid keeper, Michael Konsel, and passed for Andy to score.

During the last 20 minutes we doubled our lead when I took a corner which was flicked on by Sharpy. Derek Mountfield ducked and Trevor Steven connected at the far post to score his 16th goal of the season.

Before kick-off I was winding up my room-mate, Kevin Ratcliffe. I said to him that we needed to stop Rapid's star man, Hans Krankl, from scoring but if Rats was marking him he probably would pop one in! Well, late in the game Krankl did score.

The Austrian captain took a pass from Johann Gross to beat Neville Southall and cut our lead to 2-1. But while Rapid switched off, still celebrating Krankl's goal, we wrapped things up when I scored our third with five minutes left.

Sharpy laid the ball off to me and when the keeper Konsel came rushing out I chipped it over him into the roof of the net.

Job done!

Everton had at last got their name on a European trophy, nearly 23 years after the club had first competed in continental competition. We all felt a great sense of pride and achievement as we ran round the stadium showing the cup to our ecstatic fans.

When I got back to the dressing room Gary Stevens and I were selected by UEFA officials to undergo a drugs test by providing a urine sample.

As anyone who's been in that situation, for whatever reason, will know only too well, it can sometimes mean a long wait.

So instead of joining the rest of the lads in quaffing celebratory champagne Gary and I were shown into a small room and just had to sit there drinking water, waiting and hoping for nature to take its course.

Eventually, the water did the trick and we gave our samples. But when we got back to the dressing room to join the celebrations it was empty. The party was over!

Our tracksuits were the only things in there – everyone else was outside on the bus waiting for us before heading for the airport and our charter flight home to prepare for Wembley.

Having said that, we didn't need champagne to know what a great night it had been for Everton Football Club and, as champions of England for the first time since 1970, we were licking our lips at the exciting prospect of competing in the European Cup the following season, with a team that we felt would prove worthy challengers.

Glory Daze

Those dreams, though, would never materialise. A fortnight after our Rotterdam joy came the Heysel Disaster, claiming 39 lives, and the football world changed forever.

9

Scouse Poetry
When Norman's stormer
shattered our Treble dreams

BY common consent the Everton team of the mid-1980s under Howard Kendall was one of the finest in the club's history. It was certainly the most successful. But, for all of us involved, our trip to Wembley for the 1985 FA Cup Final was a massive disappointment because it denied us an historic treble.

We'd won the league championship in style, finishing 13 points ahead of runners-up Liverpool, with 90 points from our 42 games. In the process we also scored 88 goals, which we shared around the team.

Graeme Sharp was top scorer with 21 league goals but four others were in double figures: Trevor Steven on 12, Adrian Heath and myself on 11 and Derek Mountfield with 10, which was a remarkable total for a centre-back without the aid of penalties.

We went top in November and, apart from a short period either side of Christmas, we stayed there to the end, beating the other 21 clubs in the division at least once.

We clinched the title on May Bank Holiday Monday with a 2-0 home win over Queens Park Rangers, our 27th successive match unbeaten, to secure Everton's first championship since 1970.

So we were bouncing with confidence and belief when we went to Rotterdam 10 days later. After our convincing 3-1 victory, it was a case of 'two down and one to go' – with the FA Cup Final against Manchester United at Wembley just three days after our European triumph.

At that time, the only treble ever achieved in English football had been completed a year earlier when Joe Fagan's Liverpool lifted the league championship, the European Cup and the League Cup. Manchester United didn't land a treble until 1999.

We were also aiming to win the first league and FA

Cup 'Double' since Arsenal in 1971 by holding on to the cup we'd won by beating Watford at Wembley a year earlier. As I'd missed that final through injury it was a great feeling to anticipate that unique Wembley experience 12 months later.

So we were geared up to be history boys as we flew back from Holland in the early hours of Thursday morning, with the instruction from Howard to report to Bellefield on Friday morning.

When we re-assembled I don't think we even had a training session. We just travelled down to our pre-Wembley hotel base in Hertfordshire and had a loosener when we arrived. After a season like that you're as match fit as you're ever going to be.

Howard named the same side that had won in Rotterdam to take on Ron Atkinson's United.

It was: Neville Southall, Gary Stevens, Derek Mountfield, captain Kevin Ratcliffe and Pat Van Den Hauwe; a midfield comprising Trevor Steven, Peter Reid, Paul Bracewell and myself, with Graeme Sharp and Andy Gray up front and Alan Harper on the bench.

It was a baking hot day and the game's decisive moments were to involve the oldest and youngest players on the pitch: former Everton player John Gidman, then 31, and 20-year-old Norman Whiteside, later to join Everton.

I suppose having played a European final in mid-week must have had a negative impact on us mentally and physically but there was little between the teams, and chances were few and far between.

We went closest to scoring after only 10 minutes when a long throw from Gary Stevens was punched to the edge of the box by United goalkeeper Gary Bailey. Peter Reid volleyed it straight back on target only to see Gidman deflect his shot onto a post and away.

Years later, Gidman revealed in a City Talk radio interview just how close Peter's effort had been to putting us ahead. "The only reason I made contact with Reidy's shot was because that day I was wearing extra long studs," said Gidman. "If I'd been wearing normal size studs I wouldn't have got to the ball and it would have been in." Such are the wafer-thin margins that can sometimes mean the difference between winning and losing.

Later, an attempt by Andy Gray went narrowly over the bar while at the other end, big Neville had to be at his acrobatic best to prevent Norman Whiteside from scoring. But the game changed dramatically in the 78th minute when my Republic of Ireland team-mate,

Kevin Moran, scythed down Peter Reid as he was running clear on goal. Today, it would be a straight red card offence and accepted as such.

The disciplinary climate of 1985, though, was very different and when referee Peter Willis ordered Kevin off – making him the first player ever to be dismissed in an FA Cup Final – it was like lighting a blue touchpaper. Kevin was a friend of mine and widely respected – we certainly didn't want to see him sent off. Kevin himself was so angry at the decision that he had to be restrained by his team-mates.

Reidy, who'd been on the receiving end of Kevin's challenge, implored the referee not to send him off but Willis, a County Durham policeman, was adamant he had to go for 'serious foul play'. I can't help thinking that as it was his last game in charge, perhaps he wanted to go out having made history? Who knows. Maybe that's unfair.

So Kevin, with an unwanted place in the record books, had to make a lonely, disconsolate walk back to the dressing room and wasn't even allowed to go up the steps to the Royal Box at the end.

Ironically, Kevin's departure seemed to galvanise the ten men of United – who switched striker Frank Stapleton to a deeper role – just as perhaps we were beginning to feel some fatigue from our demanding build-up to the final.

The game moved goalless into extra-time and there were only 10 minutes left of the additional period when Norman Whiteside struck. If you're going to lose a final you never want it to be through a scrappy goal – and Norman's was far from that!

He ran onto a Mark Hughes pass out on the right, evaded Pat Van Den Hauwe and steered a precise shot past big Neville and into the net. It was spectacular and he'd directed his shot in the only place that was going to beat Neville.

It meant huge disappointment for us to miss out on a landmark treble and it put a bit of a dampener on things.

Yet it had still been the most fantastic year in Everton history, in which we set what was then an English record of 43 victories from our 63 games in all competitions, and we were delighted to be named European Team of the Year.

In addition, there were other accolades. Howard Kendall was named Manager of the Year, Neville Southall was elected Footballer of the Year and Peter Reid was voted PFA Players' Player of the Year by his fellow professionals.

Where it started: (Above) Tram Inn Hotel, Allensmore, Herefordshire – the pub where I perfected my free-kicks. Right (front, middle), with my six-a-side team

Oval ball: With my school XV, holding the wrong-shaped ball

Wing man: Turning out at Hereford's Edgar Street during a pre-match game

Hereford boys: Lining up with Hereford Under-15s (front row, centre), 1974/75

Trophy signing: (Left) Player of the tournament at an Under-14s competition and (above) signing schoolboy forms for Hereford United with my father

FANS HAVE GOOD VIEW OF SHEEDY

Hereford Utd. 1, Chelsea 2

A CROWD of 3,229 — one of Hereford's largest gates for a friendly — fully justified manager John Sillett's decision to invite his former club to Edgar Street.

Terry Paine put Steve Ritchie clear from a free-kick to open the scoring in the 20th minute and then retired from the proceedings to enable schoolboy Kevin Sheedy to have his first taste of senior football.

Sheedy, aged 16, who showed up well throughout, almost put Hereford two up with a left-footed drive which brought a fine save from goalkeeper Peter Bonetti.

Chelsea skipper Ray Wilkins equalised in the 37th minute from an Ian Britten cross.

The Second Division club snapped up the winner in the 67th minute with a goal from Ray Lewington after another Britten cross.

In the second half, Hereford brought on Dover full-back Ken Reynolds, who received special permission to play in the match.

HEREFORD UNITED FOOTBALL CLUB (1939) LIMITED

Hereford United F C   V   Chelsea F C

Tuesday 13th January 1976
K.O. 7.30 p.m.

Hereford United

From: Hughes J
Emery S
Ritchie S
Laytor J
Rylands L
Lindsay J
Paine G
Tyler D
Davey S
McNeil D
Carter R
Byrne J
Marshall J
Charlton K
Williams G
Sheedy K

Referee: R Marshall

Linesmen: D Meredith
R May

Chelsea F C

From: Bonetti
Lock
Harris
Hay
Droy
Wicks
Britton
Wilkins R
Maybank
Hutchinson
Garner
Cooke
Wilkins G
Bason
Lewington

Our thanks to Ron Suart and Eddie McCreadly and the Directors of Chelsea for allowing the side to come and play us here at such an important time in the football season and we wish them well in the next round of the F A Cup against York City.

Also our thanks to the referee and linesmen for their services this evening.

Next match: at Edgar Street

Football League: Saturday 17th January 1976

V Chesterfield F C   K.O. 3.00 P.M.

Making an impact: (Pictured top left and above) In action, and lining up with Hereford United reserves, at the age of 16. Newspaper cutting and a teamsheet signed by Peter Bonetti from a game against Second Division Chelsea – a first-team friendly at Edgar Street, January, 1976

Kevin, 16, is set to make FL debut

Dale McNeil who will be having a fitness test today.

APPRENTICE Kevin Sheedy, aged 16½, is expected to make his Third Division debut of the season against Preston North End at Edgar Street tonight and will become the youngest player ever to wear a United shirt.

Sheedy, who plays in midfield, is aged 16 years and 190 days and will beat the existing record set up by his reserve team colleague Brian Preece who was 16 years and 41 days when he made his debut against Blackburn Rovers last season.

Sheedy, who left St Mary's School, Lugwardine, at Easter and signed apprentice professional forms for the club, has been a regular reserve team player this term.

He made 15 appearances for the United side that carried off the Midland Intermediate League Championship and was substitute on five occasions.

He played four times in the Northern Floodlit League and was substitute on three occasions and also for the United first team two games against Chelsea at Edgar Street in January.

United manager John Sillett has named a squad of 13 players but will not be able to select a side until he scorer Dixie McNeil has been given a fitness test.

McNeil, who has netted 34 times for the club this season, suffered a recurrence of last night's friendly match with Bristol City, which was drawn 1-1, and was described as "extremely doubtful" by the Hereford chief this morning.

If the former Lincoln City striker is passed fit he will be bidding to score a hattrick to become the country's joint top scorer for the second successive season.

He needs three goals to draw level with Tranmere's Ronnie Moore who looks like topping the charts with his tally of 37. In second place is Walsall's Alan Buckley, who has 35 to

Player of the Year

BEFORE tonight's match Hereford United's player-coach and captain Terry Paine will receive the Player of the Year award on behalf of the team from former club vice-chairman Mr Arthur Round.

For the past 10 years Mr Round, who originally presented the trophy, has issued voting papers for supporters to nominate their outstanding player and there has always been keen competition for the award.

But this season the board of directors decided that the award should go to the team in recognition of winning the third division championship.

his credit, and McNeil is fourth.

Peter Spring, who was signed for an £8,000 fee from Luton Town after the transfer deadline, is a definite starter after Sillett obtained special permission from the Football League include him in his team.

Spring also picked Bristol last night and replaces player-manager John Sillett.

Centre-half John Lay has received a new suspension after he 20 points in booking replaced by John Lay.

John Lay hissed the last two third games with Skywest Rotherham after an eye injury again left but he has secured.

The squad is; C. Dennis, Tucker, Ritchie, Tucker, Lindsay, Carter, Davey, Tyler, Sheedy.

United will be bidding for their eighth League season after winning impressive wins against Preston side at last November.

Preston manager Caterrick has said squad of 13 playe could make chance side that beat Port at Deepdale on Satu.

Forward Keene United and England half Dave Sadler, been in and out o with injury this sea again after missing a couple of games with injury.

Busby has made strides that have previously making it difficult to ball Catterick may get the strongest si deal with the twin it McNeil and Dover settled over 30 goals them.

Midfield player Lamb, who broke the early part of his new recently, made his comeback away draw with Rother United last Wednesd he was restor Saturday but seem back into the side aj

Catterick is try obtain permission Football League to midfield player.

Being a Bull: (Above) Reports ahead of my first-team debut against Preston, April 1976

Youth experiences: Top (on the left) trophy winner with the reserves, and above (third right) with the squad ahead of a tour to Holland

First-teamer: (Middle row, second right) In my first squad shot with Hereford United, ahead of the Second Division campaign of 1976/77

Making my name: Signing in the boardroom after joining Liverpool in 1978; (below left) in action on my league bow against Birmingham nearly three years later

All smiles: (Above, right) With our shamrocks, international team-mates Ronnie Whelan and Mark Lawrenson during my Liverpool days, and a thumbs-up after signing for Everton in 1982

Early marker: Firing home the clincher at Ipswich Town in December 1982, and (below, left) taking on Luton Town's Mal Donaghy in the final away game of that season, a 5-1 win when I scored twice

Milk Cup: (Above, right) Saluting the travelling Evertonians at Aston Villa after we'd booked our place in the 1984 final, and (below) the sides following the 0-0 draw at Wembley – I'm in my training top (back row, third left) having been injured...

Double header: (From top) A rare header, the opener in the 5-0 win over title favourites Man Utd; take two – my free-kick against Ipswich and the late FA Cup semi-final free-kick leveller against Luton at Villa Park

Euro champs: (Above) The clinching third goal against Rapid Vienna in the ECWC final in Rotterdam, and (below) celebrations on the pitch, and the plane home

Two out of three: Showing off our silverware on the streets of Liverpool – the open-top bus tour of the city in May, 1985

Scouse Poetry

As a quarter of a million people on Merseyside welcomed us back from Wembley, one banner summed it all up.

'Two out of three is Scouse poetry,' it proclaimed. And it was.

IO

Inchy

Whatever the role required,
Adrian filled it like a giant

WHEN people ask me who was the best striker I
played with – and I have quite a choice of impressive
candidates – my answer is always Adrian Heath.

I had a great understanding with him. When I received the ball I knew exactly where he was going and
whether he wanted the ball played short, in behind
him or wherever he wanted it. Inchy, as he was nicknamed because of his small stature, just had such great
movement and I was on exactly the same wavelength
as him.

He arrived at Goodison seven months before I did, signed by Howard Kendall from Stoke City in January 1982 for £750,000, which was then a club record fee. Adrian had been his boot boy when Howard had played for Stoke and had told him that if ever he got the chance to join Everton he should jump at it. Now he'd made it possible.

In Adrian's first season-and-a-half at the club Everton paraded a batch of strikers as Howard juggled his attacking partnerships to try to find the most potent combination with Graeme Sharp. Alan Biley, Mick Ferguson, Peter Eastoe and David Johnson all featured to a greater or lesser extent but as the 1983/84 season unfolded, Adrian and Sharpy had become the first-choice partnership.

It was a rough ride before Christmas in what I've referred to as the 'winter of discontent', with our form and attendances nosediving. Yet through that period, Adrian still managed to impress and scored some crucial goals before he had to take on a new role.

In the November, Howard produced two master strokes, signing Andy Gray from Wolves for £250,000 and promoting Peter Reid from the reserves, almost a year after his £60,000 arrival from Bolton. When you know the game inside out like Howard you just sense that a certain type of player – in Andy's case, a battle-hardened pro – is going to benefit the team. It was a big gamble by Howard because Andy had an on-going knee problem.

But it was a calculated risk. The plan was for Andy not to train very hard – just play. And his never-say-die attitude was a catalyst that helped transform our season from gloom to glitter. Likewise, Peter Reid's combative introduction gave us more solidity in midfield. When Andy came into our team it was tailor made for his up-and-at-'em centre-forward style, with Trevor Steven on the right flank and me on the other, putting quality deliveries into the box where Andy, brave as a lion, would fly in, put his head among the boots and score goals.

One of his trademark goals I've mentioned that stands out for me was his spectacular winner in our FA Cup quarter-final victory at Notts County that season. It was 1-1 at half-time and in the opening minute of the second half we were awarded a free-kick, which I took. Andy, parallel to the pitch, connected with a diving header that flew into the net. Most players would have tried to kick the ball, certainly not risk coming to harm diving to head it. But that was Andy – fearless.

Yes, his arrival supercharged our side and it was

educational for Sharpy, who's said more than once how much he learned from his fellow Scot, who was in the tradition of crowd-thrilling Everton centre-forwards. But for Adrian it meant a big switch, dropping back from his attacking partnership with Sharpy to where his talents became valuable in a deeper, midfield role. His movement and link-up play were so influential to the side, not to mention his continuing habit of scoring crucial goals.

One of them spared us the embarrassment of going out of the Milk Cup to Oxford United, who were then in the old Division Three, two leagues below us. It may even have saved Howard's job. We went to Oxford in the quarter-final in the January and with nine minutes left we were 1-0 down and heading out of the competition, which would have been a shameful result.

That's when Adrian came to our rescue. Oxford's Kevin Brock was being pressurised by Peter Reid and as Brock turned towards his own goal, Adrian sneaked in behind another Oxford player, Malcolm Shotton. Thinking the coast was clear, Brock directed a back pass towards his goalkeeper, Steve Hardwick. But Adrian darted after it, nicked the ball, rounded the keeper and scored from a tight angle at the near post.

Inchy

It was a goal that re-energised us. We won the replay 4-1 – when I got on the scoresheet – and went all the way to the final, where we lost to Liverpool in a replay, the game I missed after being injured in the goalless first game at Wembley. While I was on the sidelines the lads built up a great sequence of results, culminating in that 2-0 win over Watford to win the FA Cup.

Adrian Heath's part in that success was massive. Another of his key goals was the only one of our extra-time FA Cup semi-final against Southampton at Highbury, a header that soared past opposing goalkeeper, Peter Shilton, but one which Adrian later revealed he hadn't properly connected with. No matter. He finished that season as our top scorer with 18 goals from 54 starts. Sharpy and myself were the only others in double figures, with 11 and 10 respectively.

Adrian started the following season, 1984/85, like a train, banging in the goals alongside Sharpy, with Andy Gray watching from the bench.

He was on the fringe of winning a first full England cap to add to his Under-21 and B recognition when his career suffered a major blow.

In a physically-fought league game against Sheffield Wednesday on the opening day of December, Adrian was stretchered off after a horror tackle by Brian Marwood that shattered his knee, tearing apart his cruciate and medial ligaments, and his cartilage.

Adrian's knee, in effect, had to be rebuilt and he was out of action until the following season, sadly missing our great winning double of league title and European Cup Winners' Cup, plus a trip to Wembley in the FA Cup Final. I'm glad to say, though, that Adrian did collect a championship medal, having made 17 appearances in which he scored 11 goals, before his season was prematurely ended.

It was a sickener for Adrian because he was playing so well. I honestly believe that if he hadn't been ruled out, Andy Gray wouldn't have got back in the team.

However, despite the high-profile signing of Gary Lineker, Adrian was back in action the following season of 1985/86, playing in midfield and attack and appearing in 50 of our 61 games, when we finished runners-up in league and FA Cup.

Adrian collected another title medal in 1987 and went on to make more than 300 Everton appearances, scoring 94 goals, before joining Spanish club Espanyol in autumn 1988, followed by spells at several English clubs, including a period in the late 1990s back at Goodison as Howard Kendall's assistant.

Inchy

After that he became head coach of Texas-based Austin Aztex and then Orlando City, when the team relocated to Florida, where he has enjoyed success. But I know his heart is still at Everton, for whom he made a giant contribution despite his lack of inches.

11

Jack Of Hearts
When a game of cards almost cost me my place against England

AS well as being in Europe with Everton, winning international caps for the Republic of Ireland also gave me the chance broaden my horizons. One early trip with the senior squad that I'll never forget was a visit to Russia.

It was October 1985 and I flew to Moscow with the squad for a World Cup qualifier with the then Soviet Union. I'd played in our two previous qualifiers, home and away against Switzerland. I scored in our 3-0 win over the Swiss at Lansdowne Road and then we drew

0-0 in Berne. I thought I'd done well in both games. So I was disappointed when the manager, Eoin Hand, named the team and I wasn't in it. I was rooming with David O'Leary on that trip and after lunch we went back to our room.

The kit man had put David's No 5 shirt on his bed and mine on my bed – No 17. I always found it difficult to switch off and sleep in the afternoon before a game and as I was lying there, suddenly the penny dropped.

Only 17 players had made the trip and it was in the days of only five substitutes. So I realised that I was the odd one out. I wasn't even going to be on the bench! So there I was, behind the Iron Curtain, and I wasn't even part of the match squad.

I jumped off the bed and angrily knocked on Eoin Hand's door. I told him he should have had the decency to tell me what he was doing face to face, rather than let me find out the way I did. I told him what I thought of him and I don't think he had an answer.

So I joined 100,000 spectators at the Lenin Stadium feeling a mixture of chill and frustration. And to compound everything we lost 2-0. Talk about coming in from the cold – I'd gone into it!

I've been all over the globe with club and country

but wherever you go you hardly see the place because you're in the football bubble: fly in, check into hotel, have a training session, return to the hotel, have an evening meal, go for a walk in the morning, play the match in the evening and fly out!

In the days when we travelled behind the Iron Curtain to Eastern Europe you couldn't wait to get home because the hotels and facilities left a lot to be desired. I have to say, though, that in my case it never got boring travelling with Everton and Ireland because both camps were full of great characters and mickey takers. Someone was always playing a prank. I was lucky, too, in that I had good regular room mates in both squads – Kevin Ratcliffe with Everton and Chris Hughton with Ireland.

I remember on one Everton trip Neville Southall and Mike Newell were in the room next to the one Rats and I were sharing. They left their door open so we crept in. They were in bed and we threw a bucket of water over them before retreating back to our room.

We knew full well that big Nev would be plotting revenge. So when we heard them leaving their room we managed to get their door open, pinch their matchday suits, put them on and got into our beds, leaving our door open.

So when they burst in with two buckets of water we suddenly flung back the sheets and told them we had their suits on. It was an effective way of stopping them in their tracks!

One other away day experience that stands out in my memory happened on the Ireland team bus as we were travelling to play England in the 1988 European Championship finals in Stuttgart's Neckar Stadium.

Just before we left the hotel the manager, Jack Charlton, announced the team and I was bitterly disappointed to learn that he'd decided to play Tony Galvin and leave me on the bench, when I had expected to be named in the starting line-up.

Tony had played a few more games than me and Jack was always loyal to his players. He explained to me that was why he'd chosen Tony but Jack assured me that my time would come and that I'd be involved as a sub. But if not being in the team for such a massive game was hard enough for me to come to terms with, what happened on the team bus made it even worse.

I was playing cards at the back with John Aldridge and Tony Cascarino when Jack walked down the bus and joined the game. Now it has to be said that while big Jack is a millionaire, he's one of the tightest men you could meet! We were playing a game called Hearts, in which the object is to hit whoever is leading with a Heart or the Queen of Spades, which is worth 50 points. This meant that in our game of 10 pence a point it was worth £5.

Jack was leading when I pulled out the Queen of Spades and placed it on Jack's card. To say he didn't take kindly to it is an understatement. "Pick that up, you little twat," was his reaction.

I said to him: "Jack, you're the leader. That's the name of the game," to which Jack, getting even angrier and redder, demanded: "Pick that card up."

I could see Aldo and Tony smirking. But I held my ground and said to Jack: "No, I won't pick it up. It's part of the game."

At this point Jack, in a really serious, threatening tone, said: "If you don't pick that card up you won't be sub today." And he wasn't joking.

But I have a stubborn streak and I told him again that I wasn't picking it up. On reflection, I was rather proud of myself that I'd stood up to him and hadn't given in, but I didn't know where it left me and my chances of being on the bench and getting on against England.

The card game finished and even when we arrived at the stadium and checked into the dressing room I still didn't know! It was only when Jack handed in the official team sheet that I found out that I was definitely a substitute.

As things turned out it was a great day for us. Ray Houghton's sixth-minute header from a headed pass by Aldo brought the game's only goal and Jack, clearly having forgotten all about the threat he made on the team bus, sent me on for the last 14 minutes in place of Tony Galvin to help secure a great victory.

The atmosphere was terrific. As we were facing players we met in league football in England it felt more like a derby game than a key international in a major tournament finals. Bobby Robson's England, with players like Gary Lineker, John Barnes, Peter Beardsley, Bryan Robson and my Everton team-mate, Gary Stevens, had fancied their chances. But we gave a disciplined display to deservedly come out on top.

The mood and spirit in our camp was terrific. It reminded me of the camaraderie we had at Everton – it was that good. Beating England was a wonderful start to the group for us and gave us great momentum as we went into our second match, against the Soviet Union in Hanover.

Jack Of Hearts

This time I started the match in the middle of midfield – the card game in Stuttgart now a distant memory – and Ronnie Whelan put us ahead late in the first half with a spectacular volley. We were leading until 15 minutes from the end when Oleg Protasov equalised.

The merit of that result was underlined by subsequent events because the Soviet side beat England 3-1 in their final group game, leaving England bottom of the table having lost all three matches.

The Soviets then saw off Italy 2-0 in the semi-final before losing 2-0 to Holland in the final, a victory sealed by Marco Van Basten's superb volley. The Dutch were undoubtedly a fine team but we ran them very close in our final group game, when we needed a draw to go through.

It was still goalless at half-time and Jack sent me on as a substitute for Celtic's Chris Morris at the start of the second half. We had a few chances and we were defending well as the Dutch really went for it.

With eight minutes left it was still 0-0 when a spinning, swerving header from Wim Kieft deceived our keeper, Packy Bonner, and squirmed out of his grasp into the net.

We were on the way home but the squad had done

Ireland proud. Jack was rightly accorded the honour of being named an 'honorary Irishman'. The big man from Ashington, Northumberland, who was at the heart of England's World Cup-winning team of 1966, has been one of football's great characters.

He wasn't great, for example, at remembering some names. Before a game against Wales at Lansdowne Road, he came into the dressing room with the Welsh team written on the back of a cigarette packet.

Then he started to look at the names and asked: "Who's this Allen Malcolm? Who does he play for?"

We said: "No Jack. It's Malcolm Allen!"

Then he said: "This Jeremy Charles – who does he play for?" We said: "He plays for Swansea."

"Well, he must be shit," said Jack.

That was the sum total of his team talk! But perhaps Jack was ahead of his time. Maybe it was a psychological ploy to play down the opposition in our minds. We won 1-0 that day so perhaps it paid dividends.

There was never any doubt that, behind it all, Jack was a shrewd character. He succeeded Eoin Hand in February 1986, an appointment which in itself had a touch of pantomime about it.

When the Football Association of Ireland met to decide on a successor to Eoin, they voted and selected

Bob Paisley, who was then a Liverpool director after retiring as their incredibly successful manager in 1983. But for reasons still shrouded in mystery and never explained, the FAI promptly had another ballot – and this time decided to offer the job to Jack.

As it transpired it was a fortuitous, if mysterious decision because, very soon after, Bob was diagnosed with the early stages of Alzheimer's Disease and could not have done the job.

But on the night the FAI decided to appoint Jack, their first problem was finding him! It was solved by another distinguished former England player, Jimmy Armfield, who at the time wrote for the *Daily Express* and 'ghosted' Jack's weekly newspaper column.

After several calls to contacts Jimmy finally managed to locate Jack to a river bank in the north-east, where he was fishing. A message was eventually delivered to him asking him to call the FAI and confirm he was taking the job, which he duly did.

He was like a breath of fresh air for Irish football. It was a great appointment. Jack was in charge for almost ten years and transformed not only Ireland's fortunes but also expectations. During his period in charge Ireland climbed to sixth in the FIFA world rankings, which is fantastic for such a small nation.

After the 1988 European Championships, Jack led Ireland to their first World Cup finals in 1990 and again in 1994, after which he was awarded the Freedom of Dublin by the city's Lord Mayor. We also narrowly missed out on Euro 92 after going unbeaten through the whole of the qualifying campaign in a group with England, Poland and Turkey. We drew home and away with England and our 13 goals scored was more than any of the other three nations. But, agonisingly, our goalless home draw with Poland cost us a ticket to the finals in Sweden.

Whereas Jack was strong, Eoin Hand, who was in charge when I made my debut as a late substitute for Tony Grealish in a 3-2 Euro 1984 qualifier defeat to Holland at Dalymount Park in October 1983, was a weak character. He went close to tournament qualification but allowed the senior players, such as Liam Brady, Frank Stapleton and Mark Lawrenson, too much licence and he paid the price. Jack, on the other hand, did things his way. He was in charge.

But, like I say, he could be forgetful. At the team hotel before a friendly against West Germany at Lansdowne Road in September 1989, Jack called me to his room and told me: "I'm not playing you today and you won't be a sub either. There's something I want to do today but you will be involved in the games we have coming up." That was it. He didn't go into any more detail but I realised later that it concerned Liam Brady, who he'd recalled to the side because Liverpool's Ray Houghton was unavailable because of a groin injury.

Ireland had won their previous 10 games at Lansdowne Road and although Frank Stapleton gave us an early lead, the Germans just overran us. We couldn't live with them in midfield and it was no surprise when Hans Dorfner equalised. I'd changed into a tracksuit to watch the game and as the Germans dominated the match, Jack was saying in the dugout that Liam couldn't do this and couldn't do that.

When the Germans scored Jack turned to me and said: "Sheeds. Get warmed up. You're going on." I was stunned. "Jack, I'm not one of the substitutes," I blurted out. "You left me out completely." In the heat of the moment he'd totally forgotten!

So, instead of me, Jack turned to Andy Townsend to replace Liam and, remarkably, we emerged with a 1-1 draw. Liam, of course, was a hero to the Irish fans and was a great, gifted player. But it was Jack's way of saying to the public: "I'm the manager and I'm doing it my way."

After the game Liam announced his international retirement but made one further and final appearance in his farewell Ireland game against Finland at Lansdowne Road the following May, in which I went on as a second-half substitute for John Byrne and scored our goal in a 1-1 draw. It was Liam's 72nd cap, then a record but a total that's since been overtaken by the likes of Damien Duff, Steve Staunton, Kevin Kilbane, Shay Given and Robbie Keane, who leads the way with 131 caps at the time of writing.

Big Jack knew what he wanted, he didn't care who he upset and he stuck to the same style and system of play, which was aimed at capitalising on the strengths of the players at his disposal, and introduced his own men into the squad. He made no apologies to those critics who claimed his playing style was too direct. He could just point to results. And his basic message to the players was: "It's my way or the highway."

Mick McCarthy, later to succeed him as manager, was a typical Jack player. He wasn't blessed with great pace but he was wholehearted, committed and a leader. He'd first played for Ireland under Eoin Hand and during that period one sportswriter wrote that Mick was so slow that he could move faster. One day the journalist arrived at the training ground after we'd finished the session to have a pre-arranged race with Mick. The writer had challenged Mick, and Eoin Hand had agreed to it. I said to him: "Mick, be careful here. If you lose the race it's going to be very embarrassing." "Don't worry," he said. "I won't lose."

So they set up the track, about 70 yards long, and off they went. The dew had left it a bit damp underfoot but, fortunately for Mick, he was wearing studs whereas the journalist was running in flat shoes. After about 40 yards they were level but Mick just beat him on the dip. It was a close run thing. "He was never going to pass me," Mick insisted, pointing with a smile to his elbow! The journalist, though, had made his point. Be that as it may, I don't think big Jack would have had any truck with such a race taking place on the Ireland training ground. And he never had any doubts about Mick's value to the team.

Two of Jack's best recruits were a reward for his homework in establishing players' qualification to play for Ireland: the Liverpool duo of John Aldridge and Ray Houghton. Aldo qualified because his maternal grandmother came from Athlone while Glasgow-born Ray wore the green thanks to his father hailing from County Donegal. They didn't do badly, did they? A total of 142 caps and 25 goals between them.

12

Chinese Whispers
From a boot in the face
to the boot of a car

THERE are certain events in life that make you cringe when you recall them and what happened on the evening of Tuesday, September 4, 1990, is one locked in my memory store. It followed a Chinese meal in Southport attended by the players and manager, Colin Harvey, which was a club tradition started by Howard Kendall years earlier.

After the manager had collected a certain amount from players' fines it would be used to pay for a team bonding meal and the kitty also covered the cost of taxis to ensure we all got home safely. The idea was that we'd all get round the table and thrash out any dressing room problems that might have arisen and so help foster team spirit.

As he left the restaurant Colin warned us all not to get into any trouble but what I didn't realise at this particular get-together was that my drinks were being tinkered with. I thought I was drinking wine with soda water, but some of the lads were replacing it with neat wine and after a while I was off my head a little bit. I ended up in the company of Martin Keown – who'd been one of Colin's big signings the previous summer at £750,000 from Aston Villa – Dave Watson and Ian Snodin.

By the time we arrived at the Red Rum Bar at the Carlton Hotel on Southport's Lord Street I was speaking double Dutch. Martin and I then had a row over football issues. I must have said something he took offence at and he pushed me over, kicked me in the face and split my eye. A fall out is one thing, but you don't expect a team-mate to kick you in the face.

Fortunately, I didn't have far to go home as I lived in Birkdale at that time. When I woke up the next morning, feeling worse for wear, I rang Colin to tell him what had happened. I told him that it was totally my fault and that if he was going to take any action it was me who should be in the firing line. I also rang the club doctor, Ian Irving, who for some reason didn't feel able to treat me. So I ended up in Fazakerley Hospital. Fortunately, one of the doctors there, who was an Evertonian, saw me and treated me.

As the incident had taken place publicly, the press quickly got hold of the story and when I arrived for training at Bellefield I said to Martin before we faced Colin: "Whatever he's going to do I take full responsibility."

When the two of us went into Colin's office I told him that it had been my fault, that I'd had too much to drink and that I'd said something I shouldn't have done. I also rang John Keith to ask him to put out an apology on my behalf in the media.

Colin said that he was fining both of us, which was only to be expected, but then Martin launched into a verbal assassination of Colin, the like of which I've not heard before or since.

By the time I was ready to leave Bellefield the press had arrived in force outside the training ground gates. They wanted a picture of my black eye, my legacy of the Southport incident, which was perfectly understandable. I was an Everton player and it was news.

You have to accept the ups and the downs when you're in the public eye. But to give the media the slip Terry Darracott, our assistant-manager, offered to drive my car out of the gates with me hidden in the boot. And that's what we did.

Terry drove out, turned left into Sandforth Road and up towards Queens Drive, where he stopped. I climbed out of the boot, into the driving seat and headed home while Terry walked back to Bellefield. As soon as they saw Terry, the media posse realised they'd been duped and that I'd been smuggled out! I doubt if any Everton player has ever had a stranger exit from the training ground than I had that day.

But as I drove home I kept on thinking about what had happened in Colin's office. I was shocked and embarrassed as Martin had laid into Colin, saying that the players didn't rate him and that he wasn't a good manager. It was just unbelievable for a player to be talking to his manager like that. And if I hadn't been there to hear it I wouldn't have believed it.

What made it worse was that Colin was under great pressure because we were bottom of the old First Division for the first time since 1959, having lost our first three games of the season.

Martin's tirade clearly stunned Colin, who just

looked bewildered. It certainly didn't help team harmony and I don't think it did my cause any good, either. I didn't have the best relationship with Colin, which I think was just a personality thing. Colin, in his book, said something similar about me, that I was a player he admired but had difficulty communicating with. But I just don't know why that should have been.

Howard Kendall, my previous boss, had been a master at man-management. Colin, who was a fine coach, didn't have that in his make-up. I think he found it difficult to relate to and communicate with players on an individual, one-to-one basis. When people talk and speculate about coaches or assistants stepping up to be managers this is a factor too often overlooked. Be that as it may, given the situation we were in, Colin certainly didn't need Martin's outburst and even today I still have a sense of unease about it.

We'd started that 1990/91 season with a 3-2 home defeat to newly-promoted Leeds United when Neville Southall, always his own man, had walked out of the dressing room at half-time – when we were 2-0 down – and gone back onto the pitch to sit against a goalpost!

Colin, who hadn't been aware that Neville had left the dressing room, fined him for his bizarre sit-in.

I was a substitute for that game after asking Colin to be transfer-listed because I felt my career needed a lift. I then got an ankle injury before Colin recalled me for our 1-0 defeat at Manchester City, with Adrian Heath scoring the goal that beat us. But, after our antics in Southport, Colin dropped Martin and I for the following Saturday's home game with Arsenal when the 1-1 draw, through a goal from Mike Newell, brought the club's first point of the season.

Less than two months later, though, Colin was sacked and back came Howard Kendall to take the management reins for the second time. It was sad the way things turned out for Colin, although it was great for Everton – and for him – that a week after being dismissed he was back as Howard's right-hand man.

Apart from the odd problem, there was always a great camaraderie at Everton.

We often did things together away from the club, such as the time a few of us dipped our toe into the world of horseracing.

You've probably heard the joke about the punter asking his friend where his horse finished in the race and receiving the reply: "It's still running."

Well, the horse I once partly owned never even

started. It was called Dan The Man but it should have been called Dan Wasn't The Man!

Ian Snodin, who was more than partial to sticking a few bob on the horses, came into the club one day and said that he'd been to see Michael O'Neil, a trainer in Lydiate, and had been offered a half share in a flat racer.

Several of us took him up and we formed a syndicate including myself and Snods, Kevin Ratcliffe, Dave Watson, Ian Wilson and Neil Pointon. For some reason I was elected secretary and opened a bank account to ensure it was all done on a business footing. Some business it turned out to be! We had to pay around £50 each a month. And when we went to the stables to see our equine acquisition, we passed a line of alert horses whose heads were sticking out of their quarters.

Eventually we came to a stable with no horse's head in view over the barrier. When we all looked in, our horse was fast asleep on the floor. One of the handlers gave it a prod up its hind quarters to wake it up. Perhaps that should have given us a clue that Dan The Man was not going to be dynamic...

We sorted out the horse's colours – blue and white, of course – and observed the racing tradition of stamping on them. Naturally we were all excited but soon the bills started rolling in...and in...and in. Training fees, vet's fees and food soon added up to a costly sum. So I had to go back to the lads to increase the monthly payments by another £50.

We had the horse for six months and we kept asking when it was going to run a race.

The trainer said he was going in for a race but then they'd found something wrong with it and it had to be withdrawn. Eventually, it was down to run in a Monday meeting at Pontefract.

We asked the boss if our syndicate could have the day off from training to see it run. He agreed, as long as we got a good result on the Saturday. We duly won the match and were all geared up to head for Pontefract when I received a phone call on the Sunday night to tell us the horse had been balloted out of the race.

I rang round the other lads and told them I'd had enough of Dan The Man. I was quitting. They all agreed they were finished with it, too. The problem was the bills were still coming in, including one for treatment to the horse's teeth! It was the best looking horse that never ran a race...

I told Michael O'Neil that we were ending our interest in the horse. But the next thing was that I got a letter from the racing authorities telling me that unless the outstanding bill of around £2,000 was paid we'd be banned for life from owning a horse.

So we all chipped in to pay it and reflected on a costly lesson. We started with dreams of partly owning a derby winner – and we ended up without even having a run for our money!

13

Captain Kev
Proud Welshman gave me stick but I'll give him a deserved accolade

I WAS fortunate at Everton to be surrounded by great players in every department of the team. There was the fantastic Neville Southall in goal, full-backs of the calibre of Gary Stevens and Pat Van Den Hauwe, a wonderfully balanced midfield thanks to the talents of men like Peter Reid, Paul Bracewell and Trevor Steven and up front, Graeme Sharp and the hugely under-rated Adrian Heath.

But the man I single out as the greatest I played with at Everton is Kevin Ratcliffe, a captain supreme.

And I say that not because he was my room-mate throughout my 10 years at the club, or because I used to get changed next to him every day for training or matches. I choose Kevin for his all-round ability as a centre-half of sheer class, and as a leader on and off the pitch. Having said that, he used to give me ear ache because I represented the shamrock rather than the daffodil.

Kevin, of course, is a proud Welshman, a distinguished captain of his country with 59 international caps to his name. I might have become his international team-mate if events had turned out differently when I was a young player with Hereford United.

I was selected for the Republic of Ireland Under-16 side, for which I was eligible through my father. My mother, Jean, was Welsh and at the time I received the call from Ireland I knew that Wales also had a game coming up.

So I rang the Welsh FA to ask if I was in their squad, to see if I had a decision to make. But their response was that they were not in the business of divulging their squad before it was officially announced. So that was it. My mind was made up for me. It was Ireland from then on. I put the phone down from talking to the Welsh FA and rang the FA of Ireland to say that

I'd be delighted to be in their squad.

The next day I received a call from the Welsh FA inviting me to be in their squad. I told them it was too late. I'd already accepted the Irish invitation. So in the end I didn't have to make a decision.

If I'd had to make a choice I honestly don't know what it would have been. But I've never, ever regretted playing for Ireland and, as fate and fortune turned out, I had the wonderful experience of playing in World Cup and European Championship finals, which I wouldn't have had with Wales. That was the ace card I always had up my sleeve whenever Kevin – or Rats as he was nicknamed – started giving me stick. And he really had no answer!

When Ireland qualified for their first major finals, the 1988 European Championship in West Germany, I went to the travel agents, picked up as many brochures on West Germany as I could and left them at Kevin's spot in the dressing room. I can't repeat Kevin's reaction. Suffice to say that the air was blue! Likewise, two years later, when Ireland qualified for the World Cup finals, I collected a mass of holiday literature on Italy and left it for him.

I have to admit, though, that I did genuinely feel sorry for Wales when they fell short of qualifying for major tournament finals, especially with their spine of Neville in goal, Kevin at the heart of defence and Ian Rush and Mark Hughes up front, with Gary Speed also a great talent coming through. I used to tell Kevin and Neville that Wales were one player short – me!

Back at Everton, Kevin was often one of a few players who tried to get in early on a matchday. But it wasn't just because he wanted to be well prepared for the game.

Unlike today, when clubs have multi sets of kit, we had just one set which went back in the wash, as they say, after each game. We all had our own numbered shirts but when it came to shorts, well, it was 'catch as catch can'. At Everton there were three pairs with a 38-inch waist and three 36-inch. The rest were 34s.

So you had to get to the ground handy to get one of the roomy pairs, which everyone wanted. In fact, if you got to the dressing room and found Neville Southall, Graeme Sharp and Kevin had arrived before you then you knew you would have to squeeze into one of the smaller sizes because those three, with their big backsides, would have grabbed the largest pairs!

Whenever I see an action shot of myself playing for Everton in those days and notice that my shorts appear to have been sprayed on, I think to myself: 'I must have been near the end of the queue that day!'

The subject of Everton kit always makes me think of one of the club's great long-serving characters, Jimmy Martin. When I arrived at Everton in 1982 Jimmy was employed as the team coach driver before Howard Kendall appointed him as kit man.

And when Colin Harvey became manager Jimmy had another important job – as Colin's grape tester! Jimmy would have the task of checking if the grapes had any pips for Colin to eat on the journey back from matches. If Colin found any he wasn't best amused, especially if we'd lost!

Getting back to the subject in hand, I can clearly say that when it came to football talent, there was no joke when Kevin was on the field. He was a special, influential figure.

He had searing pace, he was a fine tackler and good in the air, and his speed meant he could hold a high line, sweep up and play the ball back to Neville to launch another attack.

In one lighthearted exchange, typical of the banter we used to have, Kevin said to me: "'effin hell, Sheeds, you can't head the ball, you can't tackle, you've got no right foot and you've got no pace!"

I replied: "Maybe so, but when you lose your pace you'll be knackered!"

Unfortunately, that flippant remark turned out to be true because when Kevin got a few injuries it cost him his pace, which was a key quality in making him such a magnificent defender.

As for his remarks about me, I admit I wasn't a Peter Reid-type tackler or a Graeme Sharp-type header of a ball, but I wasn't as bad as some painted me. I scored five goals with my right foot and five from headers.

As well as his other attributes, Kevin had a powerful drive and desire to win.

And in a side packed with leadership qualities his own were second to none. He had a great rapport with Howard Kendall, which was a great example of a manager/captain relationship.

Kevin was Howard's voice on the pitch and any problems would soon be sorted out thanks to Kevin. He was perfect for the role, a good communicator on and off the field.

As a player he was so quick that even in the present era, when speed and athleticism are a feature of the modern game, he would be perfectly suited.

Kevin also had an inner steel. If a striker was giving him a hard time he would sort him out in a 50-50 tussle. That's definitely not something he would get away with today!

I'm not surprised he has gone on to carve out a good career in the media. He's a good talker and he knows the game inside out. What more do you need in a pundit?

14

Managing
Calling time on my Everton career
and taking the next step up

I MIGHT have gone into management if a few points on my career path had led me in slightly different directions. After joining Kevin Keegan's Newcastle United on a free transfer in 1992, ending almost a decade at Everton, I helped them win promotion to the Premier League, which had been launched the previous season, 1992/93.

When I left Everton, during Howard's second spell in charge, the team was very much in transition. In the autumn of 1991 I went out of the team with hamstring and Achilles trouble but after missing eight games I scored with a header in a 2-2 draw at Oldham Athletic in December. But I was substituted for Tony Cottee early in the second half of our next game, a 4-2 defeat at Arsenal, which turned out to be my last appearance in an Everton jersey. Howard dropped me for the next match, a 1-0 Boxing Day home defeat by Sheffield Wednesday. I wasn't even one of the two substitutes then permitted.

To prepare for the match – which was on a Thursday – we went away to a Wirral hotel where I roomed with Neville Southall, who had complained about an ankle problem but had been passed fit. When we went down for breakfast on the morning of the game I sat at a table with Peter Beagrie. Howard then came down and started to talk to Peter, saying he was going to name him as a substitute. Howard never said a word to me but later on I learned I was going to be a substitute as well. He never explained why and it riled me that while he explained to Peter the reasons he was going to be on the bench he didn't tell me.

So Peter and I were named as our two substitutes. When we got to Goodison I went into the players' lounge to sort out my match tickets but as I got back to the dressing room Colin Harvey told me that I wasn't going to be a sub after all. They'd decided to put goal-keeper Gerry Peyton on the bench as cover for Nev-ille along with Peter. So it turned out that I'd been a substitute who'd been substituted without ever getting stripped!

I was absolutely fuming as I watched the match. When I went into training the following morning, with a home game against Liverpool looming the follow-ing afternoon, our reserve-team coach Jimmy Gabriel told me that Tony Cottee had a so-called injury. Tony hadn't played very well against Sheffield Wednesday and Jimmy said there was a possibility I'd be playing in the derby. Because of that Jimmy told me to take it a bit easier in training. I told him that the manager hadn't spoken to me and unless and until that hap-pened I'd train as hard as I could.

As things turned out I wasn't selected and I never made another Everton appearance. It was a regret-table way for my Goodison playing career to end. I wasn't playing regularly and it was going to happen at some stage. It was just unfortunate the way it did.

Although I would have been eligible for a testimonial the following summer, on completion of ten years at Everton, I've never been driven by money. What I wanted was first-team football.

So when the opportunity arose to join Newcastle, managed by Kevin Keegan who'd just succeeded Ossie Ardiles, I eagerly took the chance to go to St James' Park.

I left Everton with a heavy heart. But I knew I was moving from one big club to another and it gave me a chance to work with another football great in Kevin, who was out to prove himself as a manager. Just as it was a telephone call from sportswriter Colin Wood that had told me about Howard's interest in taking me to Everton a decade earlier, it was another that alerted me to Keegan's interest. And once again I thought it was a prank!

In February 1992, I was away on international duty with Ireland at the Dublin Airport hotel, waiting to leave for a game against Wales, when there was a phone call for me. The voice said it was Terry Mc-Dermott, who was then at Newcastle. Although Terry has a distinctive lisp I still thought it was one of the Ireland lads, like Andy Townsend or Tony Cascarino, winding me up. It was the sort of thing they'd do.

But I soon realised it was Terry on the line. I'd known him from the time we were together at Liverpool. "Would you be interested in coming to Newcastle?" Terry asked me. "Of course I would," I replied.

Managing

Terry told me not to mention it to Liam O'Brien or David Kelly, two Newcastle players who were away with me for Ireland, and to travel to Newcastle for talks when I got back. I played in the international, flew back to Liverpool the next day and then drove up to speak to Kevin, who I'd never met before. There were no agents involved but he didn't need to sell Newcastle to me. I knew what a football hothouse it was. I'd played there and I knew how fervent the fans were. Even though the club was in the old Second Division, the second tier of English football, I felt sure a move there would give my career a kick. So I signed.

Nobody was more surprised than Liam O'Brien and David Kelly, from whom I'd managed to keep the secret even though I'd had a meal with them after the international in Ireland. Back home, they switched on the television evening news and there was me standing outside St James' Park draped in a Newcastle scarf after signing. They gave me a lot of stick about that!

When I arrived, Newcastle were in danger of being relegated to the old Division Three. Brian Kilcline had also been signed and we made our debuts together in a 1-1 home draw with Barnsley. I played in all but one of the remaining games, and scored to get us a crucial point in a 1-1 draw at Grimsby Town.

We stayed up by winning our last game of the season, 2-1 at Leicester City, to finish 20th in the 24-club league. That was a huge relief for the club and provided the momentum for a superb start to the 1992/93 season. We won the opening 11 league games, of which I played in nine and scored a couple of goals. Everything was going fine. I'd moved my family to the north-east, my children were in school there and with my contract due to expire at the end of that season I went in to see Kevin, to ask if he'd be offering me a new one.

He said: "You've done great for me. No problem. We'll offer you a new contract." But then he bought Scott Sellars from Leeds United and Andy Cole from Bristol City and I found that I wouldn't be getting a new contract after all, despite our verbal handshake. It left me with a very nasty taste. In two days I'd gone from being assured I had a future at Newcastle to learning there was nothing there for me. Our 3-0 victory at Tranmere Rovers at the end of February was to be my 48th and last first-team appearance for Newcastle.

Suddenly I found myself in the reserves against Bishop Auckland getting booted left, right and centre. The next day I got a telephone call from Cardiff

City manager, Eddie May, asking if I'd be interested in going there on loan. I told him I'd be delighted. But then I got another call. It was from Kevin Keegan, asking if I'd spoken to Eddie. I told him I had but Kevin said: "He's not spoken to us." I presumed he had and Keegan and I had what might be called in polite terms an exchange of pleasantries. I never got to Cardiff.

Effectively, that finished my Newcastle career. But I did leave at the end of that season with a First Division title medal after making 24 appearances and scoring three goals, as Newcastle returned to the top flight as champions with 96 points, eight ahead of runners-up West Ham United. You can't put a price on winning medals.

That summer I was approached by former Everton player and manager, Billy Bingham, to see if I fancied going to Blackpool, where he was on the board. I duly signed for them after meeting Billy and the chairman, Owen Oyston. Billy Ayre was manager and I later learned that he didn't want me there. Perhaps he saw me as a threat?

Billy made it as difficult as he could for me to play and I thought: 'What have I done wrong here?' Looking back, though, it probably did me a favour. After playing at the top, the game at the lower levels can be an unknown void. This was a valuable learning curve and, despite the problems, I made 25 league starts that season when we finished 20th in Division Two, escaping relegation by a point.

Sam Allardyce succeeded Billy as manager but he didn't seem too keen on me either, which completed an unwanted hat-trick for me after my experiences with Keegan and Ayre. Although I'd signed an initial two-year contract at Blackpool I didn't make a single appearance under Sam in my final season there, 1994/95.

In fact, you could say that Sam left me to sing for my supper – or for a football contract at least. That's what happened on an eventful trip to Hong Kong.

It happened in 1995 during the final season of my two-year stint at Blackpool. When I received an invitation to make guest appearances for a local club in a couple of games in Hong Kong I was delighted to accept, and Sam was happy for me to go.

One of the matches was against some of the great Brazilian stars of Flamengo Old Boys and before the game I was asked to go onto the pitch with Zico and Junior to take part in a televised free-kick competition. What a journey. From my formative years practising free-kicks against the wall of our family's pub, The Tram Inn, in Herefordshire, to competing against two brilliant Brazilians on the other side of the world!

We had five free-kicks each and Junior and I had scored from four of ours when Zico stepped up for his final kick – and bent it into the top corner to win a £20,000 cheque. I'd just enjoyed taking part though.

After the second match the organisers asked if I'd stay on to guest in another game. I agreed a fee of around £5,000 and the owner of the club invited me out for a meal. We ended up going to a karaoke bar. While we were there he asked me to get up and sing. Well, it has to be said, I've got the worst voice in the world, and told him so. Karaoke is huge in that part of the world after originating in Japan. Just how big I was about to discover, to my cost! The football club owner kept insisting: "You must sing." And I kept telling him I couldn't.

In the end there was nothing for it – I HAD to get up. I can't remember what I attempted to sing. I tried a duet and all I know is that it was horrendous. The football club owner took my paltry attempt as an insult. I think he felt his honour and reputation had been damaged! He told me our agreement for me to guest in another match had been terminated.

The next day I dialled the number he'd given me, to try to clarify the situation, only to hear the warning message: "Do not ring this number again."

So my exciting trip to rub shoulders with the great Brazilians had, quite literally, ended on a wrong note. Or rather, a few bad notes!

Later that year, having acquired the FA's Advanced Coaching Licence, I jumped at the chance to become a youth coach at Blackburn Rovers, which I did for a year-and-a-half. My former Everton team-mate, Alan Irvine, was Academy manager at Blackburn with another ex-Evertonian, Terry Darracott, the youth coach. But Terry had to have a knee replacement which would put him out of action for a few months, and Alan asked if I'd come in as cover for him.

It was a great way to start my coaching career because of what I learned from Alan. When Terry had recovered from his operation he took over the reserve-team coaching job, which had become available, and I became youth coach officially. It was a period that I enjoyed immensely.

But when my Republic of Ireland pal, John Aldridge, was appointed player-manager of Tranmere in April 1996 he rang me and asked if I fancied taking charge of the reserves at Prenton Park, which I did. I eventually became first-team coach and assistant-manager. Then, when Aldo resigned in March 2001 after our 3-2 home defeat by Barnsley, I was put in charge with Ray Mathias for the final 11 games before Dave Watson came in as manager.

I had a short time out of the game after leaving Tranmere but when the Chester City manager's job became vacant I applied for it. I didn't get the role but I experienced one of the funniest incidents I've ever seen which, thankfully, had a happy ending.

I drove into the stadium car park at Chester and, as I was early for the job interview I sat in the car and waited. There was a queue of people waiting to buy tickets and one man had a Jack Russell dog, which was a bit boisterous, leaping up at passers by.

The owner got a bit fed up with it so he tied the dog's lead to the bumper of an empty, parked car. The car owner came out and got into the car on the blind side of the dog owner and started the engine, quite oblivious that he would be towing a dog! The engine started up and fumes were coming out of the exhaust. But mercifully for the dog about 20 people, who saw what was happening, raced over to tell the driver he had an external passenger.

After missing out at Chester I applied to be manager at Hartlepool, not knowing that my friend and former Everton team-mate, Mike Newell, had also applied. We both got interviews and Mike was handed the job. But a fortnight later, Mike rang me to offer me the post of first-team coach, which I gladly accepted. Even though we'd applied for the same job Mike knew me well enough to know that I would give him loyal support.

It was a strange time because we were following success. The previous manager, Chris Turner, had taken Hartlepool to promotion after finishing second in Division Three but in November 2002 he was head-hunted by one of his former clubs, Sheffield Wednesday, and appointed manager at Hillsborough, hence the vacancy which led to the arrivals of Mike and myself.

As Chris had done so well we were on a hiding to nothing but I'm pleased to say that we went top and stayed there for the majority of the season. Although Rushden & Diamonds made a terrific closing run to take the title we finished runners-up, two points behind, to gain automatic promotion to the Second Division. Mike and I had done the job we'd been brought in to do but, unfortunately, there was friction between Mike and the chairman, Ken Hodcroft. That summer I was away on holiday, turning my thoughts to the new season ahead, when I got a call from Mike to tell me he'd been sacked. I also suffered the same fate. But such is football. And you move on. After that I went into business with a friend of mine but I always intended to return to football. It was something that was in my blood.

In 2006, opportunity knocked, literally out of the blue, when Everton came calling. Phil Cannon, then Everton's chief Academy scout who later became Blackburn's Academy manager, put my name forward. Everton's Academy head Ray Hall offered me the job of youth coach and I jumped at the chance.

15

Vatican Times
Italia 90: My greatest football memory
... and Jack meets The Pope

IRELAND'S eye-opening performances in the 1988 European Championships in West Germany sent us into the qualifying tournament for the 1990 World Cup Finals in Italy with a great spring in our step. We were brimming with confidence and belief.

We were grouped with Spain, Hungary, Malta and Northern Ireland, which is where we opened our campaign, with a goalless draw at Belfast's Windsor Park.

I scored in our next game, a 4-0 victory over Tunisia in a friendly at Lansdowne Road, but a groin injury in that match kept me out of the Everton team for several games. During that period I also damaged my calf, which extended my absence and ruled me out of Ireland's next qualifier, a testing trip to play group favourites Spain in Seville in November, 1988.

I was one of a batch of injured players ruled out of Jack Charlton's squad. Ronnie Whelan, Chris Hughton, Paul McGrath and David Kelly were also absent, and Jack recalled Arsenal's David O'Leary after a two-and-a-half year exile from international football. The pair hadn't spoken since Jack left David out after he'd played in the first match of the Charlton era in February, 1986. But David instantly answered Jack's call to make a daunting return in Spain.

Ireland's weakened team held out for a 0-0 half-time scoreline, but lost 2-0 through second-half goals from Manolo and the man they nicknamed 'The Vulture', Emilio Butragueno. So after our opening two group games we were next-to-bottom of the table with a single point, with only goalless and pointless Malta beneath us.

A knee injury kept me out of Ireland's next match, a goalless draw with France in a friendly at Dalymount Park, but I was back for our next qualifying game, a trip to Budapest's Nep Stadium to face Hungary.

It was essential we came home with something from Hungary and we did – a point from a goalless draw. But we knew that to reach Italia 90 we had to start putting wins on the board and our next match was massive – the return against group leaders and favourites Spain at Lansdowne Road in April, 1989.

The Lansdowne surface was notoriously uneven, thanks to its use as a rugby pitch. I'm sure that was an advantage to us and had an adverse mental affect on top teams who came to play us, although that's not to detract from the fact that we still had to go out there and do the business. But I'm sure that after Spain had trained on that bobbly, bouncy pitch the night before the game they would have gone to bed not fancying it and not looking forward to playing on it, whereas our players were familiar with it and could deal with its quirks.

As it turned out, Spain scored the game's only goal – but into their own net thanks to an own goal by Real Madrid's Michel. It gave us not only a crucial victory, but set us off on a great winning run. We beat Malta 2-0 at Lansdowne Road in our next qualifier, did the same to Hungary when they came to Dublin and when Northern Ireland visited Lansdowne Road in October 1989, we won 3-0.

Our passport to the finals was officially stamped with a 2-0 win in Malta in our final group game, thanks to two goals from Aldo, which meant we finished second in the group with 12 points, one behind Spain. It was a wonderful feeling of pride and achievement to be part of a squad that had taken the Republic to the World Cup for the first time in the country's history.

Just to reflect on the fact that we were one of the 24 nations to compete in the greatest football tournament on earth was very satisfying, even if the finals overall will be remembered more for Italia 90's soundtrack of *Nessun Dorma* than the breathtaking quality of its football.

Our build-up games to the finals saw us beat both Wales and the Soviet Union in Dublin – 1-0 in each case – then draw 1-1 at home against Finland before a goalless draw with Turkey in Izmir.

Once again, as in the European Championships two years earlier, we were drawn in the finals in the same group as England and Holland, with Egypt the other nation pitted against us.

To acclimatise for Italy we went on a two-week trip to Malta. However, it didn't help very much on that score because it rained for almost the whole fortnight! It was great, though, for what is now termed 'team bonding' and during our trip we played against Malta in front of a crowd of 800 and won 3-0, a game I sat out and watched.

I was delighted, though, when Jack named me in his team to launch our World Cup programme against England in Cagliari. And, guess what? After all the rain in Malta we faced England on a wet and windy night, very like home.

Not surprisingly, in an atmosphere reminiscent of a club derby game, it was a tight, scrappy contest and certainly not a classic confrontation. We fell behind after only eight minutes when, despite the efforts of Steve Staunton and myself, Chris Waddle delivered the ball into the box for Gary Lineker to bundle over the line. It was a typical Lineker goal and a big blow. But we showed great battling qualities and a truly unforgettable moment for me came in the 72nd minute.

Tony Cascarino battled to reach a long kick from our keeper, Packy Bonner, and the ball popped out to me. When I tried to slide a pass to put Tony through the ball was cut out by Steve McMahon. But when Steve attempted a square pass to Gary Stevens I'd read what he was going to do and intercepted it.

The England goal looked inviting and I hit the ball sweetly. Whether it's in a training session or a crucial match, you always know when you've made a telling connection. I knew as soon as the ball had left my foot that it would beat Peter Shilton. And, sure enough, it arrowed into the bottom corner of England's net. Pure joy! We were level – and I'd scored.

Not only had I scored a goal in a World Cup Finals I'd also become the first Republic player to do so. But I got a shock when I saw the television replays of the goal after the game, because Alan McLoughlin was offside. He would surely be deemed to be interfering with play because he was doing what all good attacking midfielders do by following up, ready to pounce on any rebound. Fortunately for me and Ireland, there were no appeals by England and my place in the record books was secure.

As you will read elsewhere in this book I have been fortunate to have enjoyed plenty of marvellous, unforgettable experiences with Everton and Ireland. But that goal against England was the crowning glory of my football memories.

As a young boy I sat enthralled watching World Cups on television, seeing great players score great goals and revelling in the magic of it all. So to go to a World Cup and score a landmark goal has got to be the star item in my mental scrapbook.

In the afterglow of our England result we were widely expected to win our second match, against Egypt. They were rated the also-rans of the group in their first appearance in a World Cup Finals since 1934. Yet they had held Holland 1-1 in their opening group game so they were far from an easy touch. And so it proved, as we played out a rather uneventful goalless draw in Palermo.

My only recollections of the game are that Egypt put 11 men behind the ball, which stifled us, and that I had a volley which was well saved by their goalkeeper, Ahmed Shobeir. Shobeir, who was voted the tournament's third-best goalkeeper after Luis Gabelo Conejo of Costa Rica and Argentina's Sergio Goycochea, turned up at Everton's Bellefield training ground later that summer.

Colin Harvey had asked the club's scouts to keep their eyes out for a keeper to understudy Neville Southall. Jim Emery, who scouted for Everton in Northern Ireland and was at Italia 90, recommended Shobeir. He joined up on trial and impressed so much that Everton agreed a £300,000 fee with his club, Al-Ahly. But work permit problems dashed the deal. Shobeir was clearly talented though. In Egypt's three group games in Italy he conceded only two goals.

Our 0-0 draw with Egypt brought a critical response from the Irish media and the pressure was on us as we prepared for our final group game against the Dutch four days later, also in Palermo.

The day after we'd played Egypt we had a shattering experience – but one that did us the world of good! In our hotel's plush reception area there was a superb glass boat which we were told, at 1990 values, was worth £25,000.

There was a downbeat, disappointed mood among the lads as they sat in the reception, some of them reading the stick we'd got in the papers. So our physio, Mick Byrne, a great, jovial guy, decided that he'd lift spirits in the camp with a demonstration of *The Lambeth Walk*. As he came to the line in the song, "doin' the Lambeth Walk...Oy!" his elbow caught the glass boat, which started to topple. Mick, horrified as he saw it move, made a mad dash to try to catch it. But he had no chance.

The boat crashed to the floor and shattered as we all just collapsed in uncontrollable laughter. There was uproar. It certainly wasn't what Mick had planned but, if anything could have broken the moment and lifted everyone, that was it.

The hotel manager came over ranting at Mick. The

Trophy haul: With the ECWC, FA Charity Shield and Canon League trophy ahead of the 1985/86 season

Head boy: On target, and celebrating my late equaliser against Chelsea in March 1986

Anyone for cricket? The Everton XI ahead of a charity match, July 1986

Champions again: (Clockwise from top left) Celebrating my second goal on the opening day of the 1986/87 season, 2-0 victory over Nottingham Forest; match-winner in front of a huge travelling support at Aston Villa on Easter Saturday, April 1987; blasting home a derby equaliser a week later, which prompted a unique celebration; lining up with my team-mates (back row, left) after being presented with the championship trophies following a 3-1 victory over Luton Town, May 1987

Ireland duty: (Top) With my team-mates in Sofia ahead of a European Championship qualifier against Bulgaria, 1987. Above: On the ball during Euro 88, and (right) son, Mark, wearing the same shirt at school after my World Cup goal v England in 1990

Italia 90: (Top) My equaliser against England, with Alan McLoughlin (far left) looking suspiciously offside! Above: Lining up (front, centre) ahead of the World Cup quarter-final against Italy in Rome, and (left) taking on AC Milan midfielder Roberto Donadoni

On the goals trail, 1990/91: (Clockwise from top) Opening the scoring against Sunderland, the rebound after Tony Norman had saved my spot-kick; shooting for goal against Chelsea, with my Ireland team-mate Andy Townsend jumping for cover; the match-winner following a tricky FA Cup clash with non-League Woking

The Aldo experience: On the bench with my former Republic of Ireland team-mate, as his assistant at Tranmere Rovers. Looking worried at Wolves (left) and (below) at Prenton Park, with goalkeeping coach Eric Nixon also present. (Bottom) Celebrations during the stunning 3-0 FA Cup fourth-round victory at Everton in January, 2001

Grateful to be here: (Left) Waving to the crowd ahead of the Goodison derby in 2012, following my recovery from cancer; (bottom left) surgeon Dr Paul Skaife, the man who helped save my life; (below) Mum Jean, dad Michael and my kids Lucy, Mark and Maria and (above) with my wife Joanne on a trip to Jamaica

Irish honour: With legend Liam Brady after being inducted into the IFA Hall of Fame

Greatest manager: Howard Kendall popped in to see me at Finch Farm...

angrier the manager got the more apologetic Mick became. It was a very expensive accident but the beneficial effect on us was beyond price. It swept away any sense of gloom in the camp and by the time we kicked off against Holland we were upbeat about the task we faced.

We both needed a draw to qualify for the second round but Holland, parading players of the calibre of Frank Rijkaard, Ronald Koeman, Marco Van Basten and Wim Kieft, went ahead after only 10 minutes through a goal from another of their great stars, Ruud Gullit.

Once more, though, we rose to the challenge and equalised with 19 minutes left, our goal similar to the one we'd conceded to Holland in the European Championships in West Germany two years earlier.

That time Packy Bonner had been deceived by a spinning ball. This time the Dutch keeper, Hans Van Breukelen, spilled a shot and Niall Quinn was in the right place to score and take us through to the second stage.

The final group table was headed by England on four points, us in second place on three, Holland also on three and Egypt bottom on two points. Ireland and Holland were assured of progressing but as we both had identical records, lots were drawn to establish second and third places. We secured second spot which meant that we avoided a clash with eventual World Cup winners West Germany.

Our second-round match was against the talented Romanians in Genoa. Their star was the wonderfully gifted Gheorghe Hagi, whose skills earned him the nickname 'Maradona of the Carpathians'. He had a fantastic left foot and we were well aware of the threat he presented. Hagi was the man who could win the game for them. But we did well to restrict him to three or four shots from 25 to 30 yards, a couple well saved by Packy Bonner and the others just beating the post.

But such was the Romanian playmaker's reputation that when Aldo got injured early in the match and had to be replaced by Tony Cascarino, he tried to kick Hagi as his parting shot as he went off.

It was a tense contest with few chances at either end. I remember Tony heading the ball back across to me and the keeper, Silviu Lung, got down to save my shot but it was goalless after 90 minutes and after extra-time.

So we faced a penalty shoot-out to decide who would go into the World Cup quarter-finals. What a prize! And what pressure on the penalty-takers. As our recognised taker I made up my mind right away that I'd take our first kick and I knew where I was going to put it – down the middle and high up because keepers usually elect to dive one way or the other.

In shoot-outs I think regular penalty-takers have a distinct advantage over players who seldom – if ever – are put on the spot. There's no guarantee you'll score but it's a process you're familiar with. You learn by experience.

During my Everton career I scored from 11 of 15 penalties and I also failed to score once for Ireland against Wales, when Neville Southall parried my kick and Bernie Slaven scored from the rebound. On each of those occasions I didn't find the net I changed my mind about where I was going to put the kick. So I learned the lesson – once you've decided what you're going to do, stick to it.

There were 20,000 Irish fans behind the goal the kicks were being taken at and among the supporters were my mum, dad and my first wife, Debbie. As I walked up to the spot my overriding thought was that I had to score – I just could not let down my family or Ireland.

Hagi had put Romania one-up from the first penalty and my kick went exactly as planned, straight down the middle and high over the keeper as he dived. Job done, thank goodness, and another niche for me in the record books as the first Everton player to take a penalty in a World Cup Finals shoot-out. But on the day the personal stuff was secondary to our fate as a team and after I'd scored it became nip and tuck with the penalties as the tension became as tight as a drum.

Neither Jack nor his assistant, Maurice Setters, had drawn up any pre-match list of penalty-takers in the event of a shoot-out. And I can tell you there wasn't a glut of volunteers! Having said that, even if you do make plans for penalties you don't know if certain players are going to be on the pitch at the end of extra-time, or who will fancy taking a kick when the moment occurs.

Danut Lupu scored from Romania's next kick before Ray Houghton stepped up for us and scored. So it went on...Rotariu for Romania, Andy Townsend for us and Lupescu for them. Andy Townsend talked a reluctant Tony Cascarino into taking our next kick. Fair play to him for agreeing – but it was one of the worst penalties you'll ever see! As Tony took it he kicked up a huge divot and totally mishit his shot. But fortunately the keeper dived early and the ball bobbled into the net on the opposite side.

So we were level pegging at 4-4 in the shoot-out when Packy Bonner guessed right and saved from Daniel Timofte. Advantage Ireland. If our next kick went in we were through to the quarter-finals.

The task of taking it fell to my former Ireland room-mate, David O'Leary of Arsenal. He wasn't a penalty-taker and as he walked up I said to him: "Dave, don't change your mind. Just pick your spot and hit it cleanly." He held his nerve and his kick flew into the net to spark wild celebrations for us and utter despair for Romania.

We'd gone through the emotional dryer and emerged, mentally and physically spent, with a place in the last eight and a towering collision against tournament hosts Italy in Rome five days later. But before that we had one of those experiences which, as they're happening, you know will remain with you for the rest of your life − a meeting with Pope John Paul at the Vatican.

As we were flying to Italy for the tournament one of the lads had asked big Jack what he'd feel like if we got as far as the quarter-finals. With a big beaming smile, Jack, who to my knowledge was the only non-Catholic in the entire Ireland squad of players, officials and training staff, replied: "If we manage to reach the quarter-finals I'll get you an audience with the Pope!"

Well, true to his word, he delivered on that promise and two days before playing Italy the whole party arrived at the Vatican for an audience with Pope John Paul. It was a fantastic experience, especially our conducted tour of parts of the Vatican the throngs of global visitors never see. Then we waited on a stage to meet the Pope. It was a sweltering day and as we sat there Jack told our kit man, Charlie O'Leary, he was anxious not to nod off, knowing the headlines that would prompt. As things turned out the headlines that did follow our visit were good for everyone – but with a journalistic spin.

Then, onto the stage came the Pope. As he did so, Jack pushed Charlie to the front of our party and the Pope put his arm round him leaving Charlie, in his own words, "dumbfounded."

We all gathered round and the Pope shook hands with Jack before we left and headed back through Rome to our hotel to prepare for the clash with Italy. However, in the course of writing this book, I have learned what happened next.

Apparently, the British and Irish sportswriters who'd

travelled with us were looking for an angle. They'd asked Jack what the Pope had said to him and he couldn't remember. So the press pack adjourned to a bar to discuss their plan of campaign.

One of the sportswriters said: "Why don't we say that on meeting Jack the Pope said: 'The boss.'" The idea met with unanimous and gleeful approval and so the story went round the world. Even Jack believed it. And I'm told the Vatican were so delighted at such a positive global story they were more than happy to go along with it!

Sadly, it wasn't such a happy story for me in particular and Ireland in general when we met Italy in their home fortress of Rome's Olympic Stadium. We fell victim to the man who came from nowhere to become the star of Italia 90, Salvatore 'Toto' Schillaci. We also came out on the debit side of Portuguese referee Carlos Silva Valente's decisions. Virtually every 50-50 went in favour of Italy. I'm not making that an excuse but in a game as close as it was, when almost all the decisions go against you, it does affect the balance of the match. I also came up against probably the toughest opponent of my career in Giuseppe Bergomi of Inter Milan. He would be very tight on you, barge you, knee you – a typical Italian defender.

The goal that settled our fate came late in the first half, which brought me a half-time bollocking from big Jack. I received the ball out on the left wing and instead of playing the ball in behind the defenders, which is something Jack always preached, I decided to play it to Aldo's feet. Unfortunately Franco Baresi managed to get his foot between Aldo's legs to set up a swift Italian counter-attack for Roberto Donadoni to unleash a stinging drive. Packy Bonner acrobatically parried it only for the lurking Schillaci to score with an angled shot.

As we walked off at half-time Aldo said to me: "I'm going to get a bollocking from Jack now for losing the ball." As it turned out it was me who had that honour! And Jack criticised me publicly after the match for good measure. You can still hear him on YouTube. But he also told us during the interval that as we were only a goal down we still had a chance to pull off what would have been the greatest result in Irish football history. Niall Quinn hit a post and brought one of several impressive saves from Italian goalkeeper, Walter Zenga.

We ran them all the way and attacked to the end but we just couldn't find the key to unlock the Italian defence. Like other nations in that World Cup we'd been done by Schillaci, who just a year earlier had been playing Serie B football and was the last name to be added to Italy's squad. But he won the tournament's Golden Boot with six goals and also the Golden Ball as the best player in Italia 90 before disappearing from the limelight almost as quick as he'd reached it. He said of his winner against us: "It was the hardest goal I had to score. Ireland under Jack Charlton were the most robust team we faced."

He scored again in the semi-final but Italy lost on penalties to Argentina, the same fate that befell England against West Germany. If we'd reached the semi I certainly wouldn't have discounted our chances.

With Jack waving the Irish flag we did a lap of the Olympic Stadium to say farewell and a thank you to the mass of our fans in the 73,000 crowd.

They are loyal, noisy, well behaved and whenever and wherever Ireland play they are there in their thousands. Like us, they will never forget their Italian experience in 1990.

16

On The Spot
Paying the penalty when
you don't hold your nerve...

AS I've said, it was a proud moment when I became the first player from Everton to take a spot-kick in a World Cup Finals against Romania at Italia 90. I dread to think how I'd have felt if I missed.

I took my fair share of penalties for club and country over the course of my career, so I got to understand the pressures involved first-hand. It may be eight yards wide and eight feet high but the area between posts and crossbar, which can often look so inviting, can bring a heady mixture of joy and despair.

If ever there was a classic illustration of how the mental process of penalty taking can wreak havoc with the physical act of kicking the ball from 12 yards, it was provided at Old Trafford in January, 2014, in the second leg of the Capital One Cup semi-final between Manchester United and Sunderland.

The prize of a Wembley place rested on a penalty decider after a 3-3 aggregate deadlock – and what unfolded was almost unbelievable. Ten top-flight professionals took penalties and only three stuck the ball in the net!

Those who missed or had their kicks saved included Danny Welbeck, Steven Fletcher, Adnan Januzaj, Adam Johnson and Rafael as Sunderland emerged 'triumphant' by two penalties to one.

Ironically, the night before that shoot-out I watched an FA Youth Cup match between Millwall and Sheffield United which also went to a penalty decider. But that one finished 8-7 to the Blades!

I bet that if you put those Manchester United and Sunderland players on the training ground the night after that Old Trafford game, and asked them to take penalties, most of them would score.

It's difficult to explain but I think it highlights not only the pressures involved, but also what can happen if you've got players who aren't proven penalty takers or those who don't want to be in that situation.

England have suffered from that syndrome down the years. They've won only one of seven penalty shoot-outs in World Cup and European Championship tournaments and you think of players like David Batty, Stuart Pearce, Gareth Southgate and Chris Waddle who've all failed from the spot previously.

I think there's a world of difference between taking a penalty in a shoot-out and taking one during a match. The circumstances aren't the same, not least the time factor.

When a referee awards a penalty during the game the team's appointed penalty-taker usually puts the ball on the spot and takes his kick. You haven't got long to think about it, maybe a minute or two while the referee sorts things out. You just act on instinct and you generally know what you're going to do.

With a shoot-out it can take 10 to 15 minutes after the final whistle before the first kick is taken, while the two managers and coaches sort out the running order. So the pressures are very different.

The manager wants his best penalty-takers to be first in the queue to try to make sure you stay in with a chance. If it then goes to sudden death, when you have to score either to win or to stay in, the pressure changes again.

It must be a horrible way to lose a game but, having said that, if you're going to abolish replays or at least reduce their number, I don't think there's a better way. It is far better than tossing a coin or a disc. At least taking penalties is part of football and not a lottery.

I suppose you could play until one side scores – but how long would you go on for? The 'Golden Goal' and 'Silver Goal' have both been tried and proved unsatisfactory.

As I've mentioned, my own method of taking penalties is very simple: pick your spot, don't change your mind and hit it cleanly. You've got to hold your nerve. Some people claim that you can replicate match conditions for penalty taking on the training ground. I firmly believe that you can't.

You just can't mock-up in training the enormity of a live situation in a game. No disrespect to them but I've seen players on the training ground take penalties with no bother whatsoever – but as soon as it's come to a pressure situation in a match you don't see them.

I've taken pressure penalties, quite apart from my shoot-out spot-kick at Italia 90. In the 1989 FA Cup,

On The Spot

I scored from the spot to equalise and earn us a 1-1 third round draw at West Brom. We then went on to win the replay.

In the next round at Plymouth Argyle, we were losing 1-0 when we got a penalty ten minutes from the end. I knew it was a case that if I failed to score we were out. But I put it in the net and we got a replay, which we won 4-0 and we then went on to reach Wembley.

The following season I scored an extra-time penalty to earn us a draw in an FA Cup fifth round replay against Oldham Athletic at Goodison.

I only failed to score four of the penalties I took for Everton and one of those that didn't go in – against Manchester United at Old Trafford in March 1985 – was down to the fact that I changed my mind where I was going to put it and Gary Bailey saved it.

The lesson was simple – never change your mind. That's the cardinal sin of penalty taking. If you stick to your guns, hit the ball cleanly and the keeper makes a fantastic save then you've just got to hold your hands up. Sometimes the taker can be lucky, such as when they score from the rebound off the keeper after he's saved the penalty. It happened that way for me against Sunderland at Goodison in February 1991 when I scored after Tony Norman saved my spot-kick.

The goalkeeper, of course, is in a win-win situation when he's facing a penalty. He's not expected to save it. There's no pressure on him. The taker is expected to score from 12 yards.

Some keepers, though, are better than others at facing penalties. I think it's just that they have an instinct about which way to go. It's a mind game, really, because the keepers are looking at you to see if you're giving away any signals about which side you're going to go for.

Also, with the welter of data about football now available, keepers are armed with information about club's penalty takers, which can prove more than useful.

Penalty rules have changed down the years. No longer can anyone do the stuttering and stop run-up that brought John Aldridge so much spot-kick success, nor can goalkeepers stray from their line although they can move about on it, as Bruce Grobbelaar did famously in the 1984 European Cup Final in Rome.

Another strange fact about penalty taking is the number of top strikers who are reluctant to take them. Kenny Dalglish, for instance, didn't like being put on the spot and would pay special tribute to players who did take on the penalty responsibility. You would think that players whose bread and butter is scoring goals would be confident about taking penalties. So you can have situations where players don't want to take them and others who don't want to be put on the spot having to step forward to take the kick.

There are many examples, too, of how strikers in peak scoring form have difficulty converting a spot-kick. In the Merseyside derby of January 2014 Daniel Sturridge had already scored twice when Liverpool were awarded a penalty and the team's regular taker, Steven Gerrard, handed Sturridge the ball. But instead of hitting the net Sturridge sent his kick high into the Kop, admitting afterwards that he wasn't great at taking penalties.

It just emphasises that there's a world of psychological difference between instinctive finishing in the heat of the action and the colder set-piece task of beating the goalkeeper from 12 yards.

17

Aldo's Team

Happy days with the boss who
kicked goals...and teapots!

JOHN ALDRIDGE was one of the great goalscorers
of modern times. His ability to put the ball in the net
for a batch of clubs and for the Republic of Ireland
was matched by his raw passion for the game. It's still
evident now in his role as Radio City's summariser on
Liverpool match commentaries, and I can vouch for
the fact that football gets to him emotionally.

After we'd played together for Ireland we teamed up
again. John became player-manager of Tranmere in
March, 1996, and I later joined him at Prenton Park.

What I can tell you is that he was definitely out of the 'flying tea cups' school of management. In fact, I saw him go one better than that when he booted the teapot at half-time during a match, which had the unintended consequence of scalding midfielder Nick Henry as the hot brew splashed around the dressing room.

On another occasion, when we were playing at Portsmouth, two of our other midfield players Kenny Irons and Ged Brannan felt the wrath of Aldo's tongue. All through the first half, as I was sitting on the bench next to him, he was angrily exploding with industrial language about the team's performance, calling this player and that player four-letter expletives. At half-time he vented his spleen on Kenny and Ged. "One of you is coming off," he stormed. "But I don't know which one. You've both been crap." Then he turned to me and said: "Sheeds. Get me a coin." So I dug out a coin from my trouser pocket and gave it to him. He tossed it in the air and said to Kenny: "Call it – heads or tails!"

"I'm not calling it," Kenny replied.

"Fucking call it," insisted Aldo.

Kenny duly called "heads" and Aldo said: "Right, it's tails, you're off. Alan Mahon's going on."

But the entire dressing room then had to stifle a laugh when Kenny shouted out: "But gaffer – can I have the best of three?"

I will leave Aldo's response to your imagination.

Of course, I knew what Aldo was like from international duty. One abiding memory I have happened in the BJK Inonu Stadium, Istanbul, in November 1991, where we both played for Ireland in a European Championship qualifier against Turkey. We had to win to have any chance of qualifying for Euro 92, and we responded to the challenge. We went out into a hostile atmosphere in front of a 42,000 crowd and beat Turkey 3-1, despite manager Jack Charlton's selection options being shredded.

Due to injury, 17 players were unavailable to Jack, with the absentees including Ronnie Whelan, Andy Townsend, Roy Keane, Ray Houghton, Niall Quinn and Denis Irwin. But we got a great result, with two of our goals coming from Sunderland's John Byrne and the other being scored by Tony Cascarino, who partnered Aldo up front.

When we got back to the dressing room we changed into our tracksuits. We were just waiting for the police to give us security clearance to leave the stadium and board the team bus when Aldo suddenly shouted:

"The robbing bastards – someone's stolen my watch!" Aldo then goes into the corridor and starts shouting "robber" at the bloke who'd been looking after our dressing room and who we'd met before the game. The police then frogmarched this guy away. Aldo, furious and wound-up, came back to the dressing room and sat down. A few minutes later he suddenly starts laughing and announced to one and all that he'd found his watch in the lining of his tracksuit bottoms. We never did find out what happened to the poor guy who'd been falsely arrested...

Although John and his watch were reunited, time sadly ran out that day on our European qualifying hopes. Despite our great win with a vastly depleted squad, a late Gary Lineker equaliser in Poland took England through at our expense to the following summer's finals in Sweden.

Some years later, working alongside Aldo at Tranmere was a great experience for me. I'd acquired the FA's Advanced Coaching Licence and been youth coach at Blackburn Rovers when I went to Tranmere in the summer of 1996, initially as reserve-team manager. After several months Aldo appointed me assistant-manager and first-team coach and he left all the coaching to me. It was an opportunity I thoroughly enjoyed, and it was an invaluable period for me. Aldo still thought of himself as a top player and, to be fair to him, he could still do it on the field, even when he was manager, joining in the five-a-sides and scoring goals galore.

During our time together at Tranmere there were some great nights and wonderful results at Prenton Park, and our cup exploits became famous. We twice reached the FA Cup quarter-final, losing 4-2 to Liverpool and 3-2 to Newcastle, and reached the League Cup Final against Leicester in 2000. We lost 2-1 but had the distinction of being the last Merseyside club to play at the old Wembley. For a club like Tranmere it was a golden era.

We created a psychological factor about Tranmere. Teams feared coming to Prenton Park in cup competitions. Regrettably, though, the players were unable to transfer their cup form into league games. We saw the heights Tranmere could reach and we had excitement provided by players such as Andy Parkinson, who played out of his skin and scored some great goals and Dave Challinor, whose long throws were matched only by Rory Delap.

Dave's throws were a massive weapon for us and I used to ensure that all the balls were pumped to the same pressure. I'd take them into the referee's room before matches so he could check them. As soon as the ball went out of play we had another, ready to be wiped with a towel if necessary, and sent straight on for Dave to deliver his personal 'Exocet' missile. Although the opposition players would have been warned about the length of Dave's throws, I bet many of them either didn't believe it or take it on board. But they certainly did when the ball flew over their heads into the goalmouth!

Saturday, January 8, 2000, saw one of the great results in the FA Cup history of Tranmere Rovers – but every time I think of it I break out in a cold sweat because of a bizarre sequence of events.

We were drawn to play Sunderland in the fourth round at Prenton Park. It was a big game for us. Sunderland, then managed by my former Everton pal, Peter Reid, with another Goodison team-mate, Adrian Heath, his assistant, were lying fourth in the Premier League whereas we were 13th, a league below, then known as the First Division.

One of our biggest crowds of the season, almost 15,500 packed into Prenton Park and our fans were rewarded when a shot from Wayne Allison, who was affectionately known as 'The Chief', put us ahead after 25 minutes. "The ball bobbled about 15 times before it crossed the line," was how Wayne described his goal. But in a typical cut-and-thrust cup tie, his 'bobbler' still separated the teams as the game reached the 90th minute. That's when the fun started, although it seemed nothing like that at the time.

It began when our centre-half, Clint Hill, who'd already been booked, was given a second yellow card for dissent by referee Rob Harris.

My immediate response was to get another defender on. We'd already made two substitutions, Alan Mahon replacing Jason Koumas and Scott Taylor going on for David Kelly.

When making substitutions in those days you had to mark on a card, held by the fourth official, the shirt numbers of the player coming off and that of his replacement. With Hill sent off, I asked Reuben Hazell, another centre-half, to quickly get ready to go on in place of midfielder Andy Parkinson because we knew that from the free-kick awarded for Hill's foul, Sunderland would plant the ball in our box to try to salvage a draw and a replay. But when Reuben removed his sweatshirt he realised he'd forgotten to put on his number 30 jersey. He'd left it in the dressing room.

I couldn't believe it! So, instead, I turned to another defender, Stephen Frail, and told him he was going on. I duly wrote his number 18 and the number 14 of Parkinson, who he was replacing, on the official card.

But for some inexplicable reason, the fourth official wrote down number 6 – Hill's number – as the one being substituted, when in fact he'd been sent off. The next thing I see is the fourth official holding up the board displaying number 6 coming off and number 18, Stephen Frail, going on, and the game continued.

So we're now into stoppage time in the crazy situation of having 11 men on the field, despite having one sent off! Stephen Frail, the player we'd just sent on, headed out Sunderland's free-kick to concede a corner as I tried desperately to stop the game.

Finally, I managed to attract the referee's attention, told him what had happened and Parkinson then came off, correctly reducing us to ten men. But I think the referee flapped a bit in the situation and blew for full-time almost immediately, with us 1-0 winners.

Needless to say, there was a bit of commotion about the circumstances of those closing minutes, with Sunderland obviously seeing an opportunity for the game to be re-staged, although neither Peter nor Adrian said anything about it to me.

Aldo left the matter in my hands and I went straight to the match officials' dressing room. But they wouldn't let me in, at least not for half an hour or so. So I stood outside the door, waiting, and I could hear them talking.

One of them said: "We've made a mistake. The best thing we can do is just get out of here." Then I heard another voice say: "What about our expenses?" It was like something out of Fred Karno's Circus.

Eventually, I got in and asked for them to show me the substitution card, which they did. The first two entries, in my writing in black ink, were correct. But the third one had been changed in a different coloured ink from mine to make it appear that I'd made the mistake over our third substitution.

I was seething that they'd doctored the card and it put me under massive pressure. I felt my job was on the line. Television programmes were using archive footage of incidents in other games to back the media assertion that the game would have to be replayed.

The Football Association mounted an immediate investigation and the next day I had to go through the whole match video of the game and present them with a report, in which I informed them about what had happened with the substitution cards. The video also

Kevin Sheedy

showed that the wrong numbers had been displayed on the boards for our first two substitutions.

I felt that if the FA backed the match officials and not me then I would have had to resign because the buck stopped with me. But on the Monday, the FA announced that the result stood and that we'd done nothing wrong. Justice had been done.

It dispelled the lingering cloud over our victory and meant that we really could celebrate our passage into the fifth round in which we went to Fulham and came away with a 2-1 win, taking us into the quarter-final for the first time in Tranmere's history.

Sadly, we lost by the odd goal in five against Premier League opponents Newcastle United at Prenton Park. That game was followed a week later by Tranmere's big Wembley experience.

The Worthington Cup Final against Premier League club Leicester City was Rovers' first ever appearance in a major final. We didn't lift the trophy but whatever the result, it was certainly a ground-breaking season for Tranmere.

Another memorable game from my time at Rovers came against my past and present club, Everton, in the FA Cup fourth round at Goodison Park.

Aldo's Team

The date was Saturday, January 27, 2001 and it's arguably the proudest result in Rovers' history. Everton 0, Tranmere Rovers 3 was a scoreline that rocked English football.

Obviously, I'm a fervent Evertonian but when you're assistant manager and coach of a team playing against them, you have to be strictly professional and do your best for the club paying your wages. It was great to go back to Goodison and, in all honesty, nobody could have anticipated the unfolding events.

Everton went into the game sixth from bottom of the Premier League while we were fourth from bottom of the then First Division. The teams were:

Everton: Myhre; S.Watson, Xavier, Ball, Unsworth (Gough, 46); Gemmill, Gravesen, Pembridge, S.Hughes (Moore, 46); Campbell, Cadamarteri (Tal, 71). Tranmere: Achterberg; Hinds, Allen, Jobson, Hill, Yates; Flynn (Henry, 84), Koumas, Hamilton; Parkinson (Taylor, 86), Rideout (Hume, 81).

I remember Everton starting really well but then we began to come into the game and took the lead after 22 minutes when Steve Yates scored with a looping header from Sean Flynn's cross.

Jason Koumas made it 2-0 before half-time and, almost unbelievably, Steve Yates connected with a

Koumas corner for his second goal of the game to make it 3-0 shortly after the hour mark.

Needless to say, Tranmere supporters were ecstatic and we were pleased with how the team had gone about their job and upset the odds. But I remember Aldo and I saying to each other: "That's it now. We've won it – let the whistle blow and be done with it." We both had too much respect for Everton to want to revel in what was a painful experience for them and their manager, Walter Smith.

That epic win took us into the fifth round and a goalless draw at Glenn Hoddle's Southampton which set up a Prenton Park replay that has become ingrained in the folklore of Tranmere Rovers. Trailing 3-0 at half-time we seemed down and out, but a fantastic second-half hat-trick from Paul Rideout, captaining the team for the first time against one of his former clubs, wiped out the visitors' lead before Stuart Barlow snatched the winner eight minutes from the end.

It was an amazing display and the first time in FA Cup history that a team had come back from 3-0 down to win. It was also the seventh time in 16 months that we'd beaten a Premier League club after our wins over Leeds, Sunderland, Middlesbrough, West Ham, Coventry and Everton.

Aldo's Team

We went out to eventual cup winners, Liverpool, in the quarter-final at Prenton Park, and in the league we slipped down to the bottom of the table.

It reached a climax for Aldo on St Patrick's Day, March 17, when we lost a 2-0 lead at home to Barnsley and were beaten 3-2 through an injury-time goal by Isaiah Rankin. Aldo decided that was it. He'd had enough and he resigned as manager.

I tried to persuade him just to take a break and then come back and pick up the reins again. But he was adamant that after ten years at Tranmere as player and manager it was time to go. I think his health was being affected.

The club chairwoman, Lorraine Rogers, asked Ray Mathias and myself to take charge for the final 11 games of that 2000/01 season, which we did. But we couldn't stop the rot and Tranmere were relegated after ten years in the second tier. I left the club and Dave Watson came in.

After five years, at that stage of my life, it was the right time for me to move on but I'd learned so much during my period there.

I look back on my days at Tranmere with happy memories – and more than a few smiles when I think of Aldo.

18

Dream Academy
Nurturing the next generation and guarding against 21st century perils

THE greatest asset of any football club is not its stadium, its swish executive boxes or the latest sponsorship deal, critically important though all of these are. It is the depth and quality of the playing staff and the flow of new, young talent coursing through the arteries of the club.

When I returned to Everton in 2006 as an Academy coach in charge of the Under-18 team, the challenge of helping to fuel that supply line was one I relished.

As I've mentioned, Phil Cannon, who was then

Everton's chief Academy scout before joining Blackburn Rovers, knew of my great desire to get back to the Blues and he put my name forward to the late Gary Ablett, who was a youth coach at the club.

Shortly after, Gary left to become reserve team coach at Liverpool and I spoke to Academy manager, Ray Hall, who offered me the job. Needless to say, I was delighted to accept and be back at Everton – my club – once again, and to be working with young players.

There's great personal fulfilment in seeing lads who've arrived at seven or eight years old putting in a lot of hard work, climbing the football ladder and emerging as potential first team material.

To me, that's the be-all and end-all of the job, cultivating raw, young talent into players who are good enough to appear at senior level.

Everton can point to a very impressive record of doing exactly that. Ray Hall, who was in charge of Everton's youth system for two decades, oversaw the development of more than 30 youngsters to graduate as first-team players with Everton.

Not all of them had long senior careers at Goodison, but those who didn't went on to ply their trade at other clubs. So the aim of honing young talent to Football League standard had been achieved.

Dream Academy

All of us involved at youth level at Everton are driving to maintain that through-put. We are aware that players like Wayne Rooney, Tony Hibbert and Richard Dunne, who all emerged from the club's youth system, are not going to come along every day, even every season.

But if youngsters are not up to Everton's required standard our job is to prepare them to play league football at a lower level.

I think sometimes this is where the public can become confused. Because they might not see a large sprinkling of players coming all the way through the ranks to appear in the first team they think the youth system is failing.

Far from it. We're in the business – and it IS a business – of moulding and shaping football talent, given that it's there in the first place. And if we don't achieve the aim of guiding a youngster through to our first team then he can be sold on to a club lower down the scale.

Some of the lads who join us at a young age fall out of love with football. In that situation some parents, perhaps carried away by the prospect of money and fame and with pound signs in their eyes, can be pushy and try to keep the youngsters pursuing a career in the game when they just don't want to be there. It's just not fair on the kids. They should be there only if they want to be there. We endeavour to make the Academy environment as happy and stable as it can be for them. And the majority love being there.

But we can recognise by their body language those youngsters who are unsettled. So we'll have a good talk with them and perhaps suggest they leave and maybe return at a later date.

One of the criticisms of the current system is that the youngsters play matches only against others of the same age and so don't get the sometimes painful, sink or swim exposure of youngsters in open-age leagues before the advent of Academies.

I think there are two schools of thought on that. Speaking from my own experience when I was 15, I was playing for Hereford United reserves in a man's league – and it toughened me up.

Now there are no open-age leagues for Academy players and that, some people say, allows the youngsters to express themselves without the pressure, and even fear, that open-age football might generate.

There's an old saying in the game that if a player's good enough he's old enough. Personally, I feel that if a player's got what it takes he can play at any level.

Dream Academy

If Academy players progress and go out on loan to further their development they will then face hardened professionals and have to stand up for themselves.

It's an interesting debate but we have to operate within the current framework and its protective environment.

The role of a youth coach has changed so much over the years. When I was a player, the only pills I took were prescribed by the team doctor, either to combat a cold or flu or to help me get a sound sleep in the build-up to a match, both in club football and with Ireland. Now, in the 21st century, in the age of drugs, social media and mobile phones, youth coaches have critical responsibilities which were never on the horizon of their predecessors even 20 years ago.

Youngsters today have a barrage of temptations laid before them, including peer pressure. Drugs, if not freely available, are only too easily accessible. Gambling can be another scourge while the social revolution, triggered by the internet, is the biggest in living memory.

When young, aspiring players arrive at a club, they generally have stars in their eyes. And there's nothing wrong with ambition.

But they come from a generation immersed in a wave of potential perils which can wreck their careers. Football cannot escape its own society.

Football at the top level has random drug tests carried out and there are calls for these to be done more frequently. As I recalled in an earlier chapter I was selected for a random test after Everton's glorious Cup Winners' Cup final win in Rotterdam in 1985.

Yes, the waiting involved did put a dampener on my evening but it is totally right and proper that this policy is carried out in a relentless battle to keep the game drug-free. I have to say that at Academy level, though, there seems to have been a dropping off in the number of random tests in recent seasons.

I am strongly in favour of young players being randomly selected for drugs tests because if they do have a problem and it can be detected early then, as a club, we can do something to solve it. If a youngster has a drugs problem that's not discovered at an early age it will almost certainly worsen until it becomes health and career threatening. If that happens it's a tragedy.

We have to keep the dangers on their agenda. We preach to them about good habits and repeatedly tell them the crucial importance of living healthy lives and to be as fit as possible. Without that, a young player's ability will never be fulfilled and their talent will go to waste.

Coaches who mentored youngsters up to the late stages of the 20th century worked in an age without mobile phones. Now we have the internet revolution with e-mails, Twitter, Facebook and all the rest of the technological paraphernalia. It's an amazing social development which has shrunk the world and brought mass benefits. But hand in hand with that go dangers which demand responsibilities. Anyone with a phone or connected keyboard can send a message around the world in a few seconds. And once it's out there it stays out there.

With that kind of power, the constant danger is of acting in haste and repenting at leisure and, sadly, we've seen media-highlighted cases of players – some, regretfully, experienced, high-profile stars – falling into that trap.

At Everton we educate our young players in the way to behave on social media, instilling them with their responsibilities and reminding them of the pitfalls that can lie in wait for them in life generally. It's the 21st century and we have to meet it head on.

19

Dunc

From fearsome centre-forward to
preacher of passing football

HE was hailed by his manager, Joe Royle, as "un-
playable." Opposing defenders quaked in their boots
when he faced them in the box hunting goals. And the
Goodison fans elevated him to a folk hero status still
evident today on his rare public appearances.

But I have come to know a different Duncan Ferguson from the muck and bullets archetypal British
centre forward, who sometimes made the wrong kind
of headlines during his two spells at Everton between
1994 and 2006, in which he scored 72 goals in 273

first-team appearances. I had never met Duncan until he walked into Everton's Finch Farm training headquarters a few years ago, keen to coach and acquire his necessary badges. Manager David Moyes made his fellow Scot very welcome, which was beneficial not only to Duncan but also to the club as a public relations coup, given the esteem in which Duncan is held by the supporters.

To gain experience Duncan started working alongside me, assisting in the coaching and running of the Under-18 team. I knew Duncan only by reputation and, of course, from what he had done for Everton on the field. I take people as I find them and Duncan and I get on very well together. I think he's surprised a few people with his commitment to coaching and his football philosophy in encouraging aspiring young players.

He came in, worked with all the age groups and really knuckled down to getting his badges. He got through the procedure very quickly before starting his two-year course for the UEFA Pro Licence, which is the highest coaching qualification available.

Duncan is massively enthusiastic and we worked well together. He's definitely got a bug for the game. And we have similar ideas about how the game should be played. Put simply, we want the players to play football and sometimes it's total football, trying to get the youngsters playing from the back under pressure. In doing that they will make mistakes – but that's the only way they're going to learn. Playing that way they're going to get more touches of the ball, and that's the way we feel is best for their development.

The easiest thing in the world is to get a big, tall striker in and let the goalkeeper kick the ball long, aiming for him. Duncan, of course, was exactly that as a player – a big, tall striker who was hugely effective, often spectacularly so. But as a coach he's at one with me in that we both want young players to play it on the floor. The 'new' managers like Roberto Martinez and Brendan Rodgers all have their teams playing football from the back.

Obviously there are times in games when you have to adapt and maybe hit a long pass or play the ball in the air. As somebody once said, 'it's not the long ball or the short ball but the right ball'.

Overall, though, as a coach you have your principles and philosophies on how the game should be played and when you get the opportunity, you try to put them into practice. There's no prescribed right way or wrong way of playing football.

Managers, coaches and players have different opinions. But I would far rather watch the passing teams of today than, say, Wimbledon of 25 years ago. And it's from that standpoint that Duncan and I have approached the job of mentoring Everton's young players.

Duncan made such an impact as a youth coach that manager Roberto Martinez promoted him to the first team set up in February, 2014.

It was a great decision by Roberto because he knew that by adding Duncan to the senior side's coaching team he was bringing in somebody who has Everton in his DNA.

Every now and then a player arrives at a club who strikes up an immediate rapport with the supporters. Sometimes the reasons are not evident but when Duncan arrived at Goodison in the mid-1990s there was no doubt as to why the fans instantly took him to their hearts.

He had a fierce winning attitude in a centre-forward role that is steeped in Goodison tradition, a heritage forged by men like Dixie Dean, Tommy Lawton, Dave Hickson, Joe Royle, Bob Latchford and Graeme Sharp.

I know that the feeling the fans have for Duncan is

mutual. He calls them "special people." He has taken to coaching with an enthusiasm and dedication you can only applaud.

He knuckled down, got his coaching badges and I'm sure his presence and personality around the first team will be positive and beneficial.

20

The Enemy Within

My biggest victory came
without a football in sight

DURING the summer of 2012, with Britain in the grip of Olympic fever, I was given the news that sent a chill down my spine. I was told I had bowel cancer.

I sat with my wife, Joanne, in a room at Liverpool's Aintree Hospital to be told the medical diagnosis following the results of a series of tests. I would need surgery and probably lengthy follow-up treatment.

To be honest, most of what was said passed right over my head. When you hear the word 'cancer' your mind does a re-wind – memories of childhood, my football career and, most important, my family from my first marriage to Debbie: Mark, Lucy and Maria.

My parents were also uppermost in my thoughts. My mum, Jean, had tragically died with bowel cancer after it had been mis-diagnosed as irritable bowel syndrome, the same fate that sadly befell the great Bobby Moore. To see my mum suffer like that was dreadful.

And my dad, Michael, also contracted bowel cancer but after a successful operation he has, thank God, made a full recovery. I suppose at the back of my mind there was a thought that because my mum and dad had suffered from bowel cancer that I was also at risk. But it's not something you dwell on too much.

The latest NHS statistics show that about one in 15 men and one in 19 women in the United Kingdom will develop bowel cancer during their lifetime. It's the third most common cancer in the country, causing more than 16,000 deaths annually. But as I sat in that hospital room with Joanne I hung on to one optimistic phrase from the medical diagnosis and my natural positivity kicked in. I've always been a mentally tough person. Back to my days at Liverpool when things didn't go well for me but I gritted my teeth and saw it through.

I've always believed in myself and when this, the

biggest fight of my life was presented to me, I was determined I was going to win. I pledged to myself and anyone else who cared to listen: "I'm going to beat this disease." Negativity was not on my radar.

I realised that I needed medical advice when I started to make frequent visits to the toilet. Joanne even joked that I was costing us a fortune in loo rolls! But, having seen awareness campaigns in the media, when I discovered I was passing blood we both knew that it was essential to get it checked out. I was sitting on the toilet one day and I said to myself: 'I've got to do something about this'.

I went to my GP and had blood and stool sample tests, which were both clear. But my doctor said that to be on the safe side he'd send me for a camera test, which is only a slightly discomforting procedure and nothing to be afraid of.

What a good decision that proved to be. The camera test was a worrying procedure. I could see my insides up there on the screen and they took one tissue sample after another. That made the alarm bells ring. I thought: 'They're excavating in there!' They were telling me nothing while this was going on. When it was over I was sent back to the waiting room. That was a scary time for me.

All the other people in there eventually went through to see the specialist, leaving Joanne and me on our own, waiting and wondering, my anxiety growing. Even a second set of people came in and left, apart from one lady who told us that she had a friend who'd had a test which revealed she had terminal cancer. It is hardly the thing you want to hear in that situation.

Finally, after about an hour and a half, which seemed like an eternity, Joanne and I were called into a room with a couple of nurses. I could tell by the looks on their faces and the silence that it wasn't going to be good news.

I sat down and they told me they'd found a tumour. But they said that if you were going to develop a tumour then this one was in a good place for removal. I seized on that mentally. That was the positive clamp of my determination to beat it. I have no recollection of whatever else was said in that room.

About a week later when I saw the surgeon, Paul Skaife, he re-iterated that the tumour was accessible for surgery, which gave me even more re-assurance. He also told me that for polyps to develop into tumours took about seven or eight years, which was something I just couldn't take in because I had no symptoms then. The fact that he told me he would operate in three weeks also raised my spirits. I wasn't being rushed in as a dire emergency.

So I went back to work at Everton, which took my mind off things, before going into hospital for surgery in late August. I sat in my room the day before the operation and that's when I began to think deeply about my situation. I went into a little bit of a bad place mentally, but I was saved by the fact that the television in my room had broken.

I wanted to watch the live screening of Liverpool's Europa League game at Hearts that night so it meant going into a communal room to watch it with a lot of other lads. We had a bit of banter and when I got talking to them I realised that so many of them had much more serious conditions than I had. It put things into perspective for me.

I went back to my room after the match and the following morning I had the operation. I hadn't read the pre-operation literature. My view was that they were going to do what they were going to do.

As I came round after the operation, Joanne was at my bedside with some nurses. One of them, Mark, who had given me plenty of encouragement the night before, was among them. He was a great character and told me: "Fantastic news. They've found the tumour. They've taken it out and you don't need a bag."

I didn't know what state my nether regions were in so Mark moved the blanket for me, had a look and shouted: "They've taken your cock off!" Cue laughter all round from the nurses and my wife.

That bit of Scouse humour was my first medicine. And when I saw Mr Skaife he confirmed that the tumour had been removed and they'd sent it off to be tested. He also had more great news – as well as not needing to wear a bag, I didn't need chemotherapy or radiotherapy. I was expecting all of that, so to learn I didn't need it was so uplifting.

I was hitched up to a drip but the nurses soon got me back on my feet, walking up and down the corridor. I got stronger by the day and once I'd shown that everything was back in working order by going to the toilet without any problems, I was allowed to return home only a week after the operation.

It was a massive relief that everything had gone so smoothly and, frankly, a little bit surreal that it had all been so quick. The NHS comes in for much criticism but I cannot speak too highly about Mr Skaife, his team and the staff on Ward 4 at Aintree. They saved my life and gave me the best treatment and on-going support I could ever have wished for.

Mr Skaife said I'd probably need to take about three months off for recuperation but I ended up going back into Finch Farm ten weeks later to ease myself back in and link up again with my fellow youth coaches, Neil Dewsnip and Duncan Ferguson, who had held the fort superbly during my absence.

They say that every cloud has a silver lining and the fact that I've managed a full recovery has provided exactly that. The publicity my illness attracted has been a great boost to heighten public awareness that the disease can be beaten and the critical importance of early diagnosis, which has been emphasised by a national age-related bowel cancer screening programme. I was also delighted to receive letters from people telling me that when they read about my situation they recognised symptoms in themselves, and subsequently went to their GP.

Early diagnosis is essential. That's the crucial message to get across. If someone isn't sure they must go to their doctor. Don't be embarrassed, otherwise you could die of that embarrassment. In general, men are more resistant than women to consulting their GP. But it's crucial they remove such self-imposed reluctance. I'm told that more than 90 per cent of people who are diagnosed at the earliest stage are successfully treated so the message is crystal clear. Surgical skills in dealing with bowel cancer have advanced to such a degree that the success rate has vastly improved and I would appeal to anyone who suspects they have the disease to take action.

Help is also available online at: **bowelcanceruk. org.uk** (telephone 0800 840 3540) and **beating-bowelcancer.org** (telephone: 08450 719301). Age-related bowel cancer screening kits are also available by calling Freephone 0800 707 6060.

I'd also like to thank people for the unbelievably huge number of 'get well' messages I received from all over the world. I got one letter from an 80-year-old grandmother who told me that she'd recovered from bowel cancer and was in fine fettle.

One of the many encouraging telephone calls I received was from Craig Johnston in Australia. I was at Liverpool with Craig and he went to the trouble of finding my number and calling me.

I was very touched by all the good wishes, just as I was when Everton invited me to walk out to the centre-circle at Goodison prior to kick-off in the Mersey derby in October 2012, shortly after I'd returned to work. To hear the ovation from both Blues and Reds supporters was a wonderful, emotional experience for me and when I stood there, I was conveying the message that bowel cancer is beatable.

Arising from my cancer operation I became involved with the Bobby Moore Fund for Cancer Research UK. Bobby's widow, Stephanie, asked if I would support a few functions to support the campaign, which has been set up to raise awareness and funds for key research into bowel cancer, which tragically took Bobby's life at the age of only 51 in 1993.

I was a Wembley guest of the Football Association at England's friendly against the Republic of Ireland in May 2013, and was delighted to do a television interview about the disease and stress the importance of early diagnosis.

It was great to be at an Ireland game again and the team deserved their 1-1 draw. The match came just three months after I'd received the honour of being inducted into the Republic of Ireland's Hall of Fame by the Football Association of Ireland.

It was a real thrill to be considered officially one of Ireland's greatest players and my name was added to the prestigious list at an awards ceremony in Dublin, which was screened live on Ireland's national television service, RTE.

I felt proud to follow great Irish players such as Paul McGrath, David O'Leary, Kevin Moran and a winger older Evertonians hold in high esteem, Tommy Eglington, among other legendary names.

I played for Ireland for 19 years, from the national youth team and Under-21s before winning 46 full caps and playing in World Cups and European Championships, which I've talked about in depth in other chapters.

So a season which had begun for me with high personal anxiety after my cancer diagnosis ended on a wonderfully satisfying note. Thanks to medical skill and personal determination I'd beaten a threatening disease, resumed my job at Everton and been given a wonderful award by the country to which I'd committed my football allegiance as a 16-year-old.

I also feel honoured to be made the first ever Ambassador for Beating Bowel Cancer, a charity I've been working with which supports all those affected by the condition. It improves awareness and promotes early diagnosis.

Since my recovery I've participated in a number of media interviews with the charity, to make people more aware of bowel cancer symptoms and to help spread the word. I'll be working alongside Beating

The Enemy Within

Bowel Cancer to help promote their campaigns and activities to ensure that more people are diagnosed at an early stage.

The perspective of my life has changed in a very short time. Bill Shankly once said that to walk out onto the grass in the sunshine with a ball at your feet was a wonderful feeling. I now know exactly what he meant.

21

The Greatest

I was privileged to share the field with
some magnificent players

NOW here's a quiz question for you. When was I, a
Republic of Ireland international, called into a squad
by England manager Bobby Robson?

Well, it happened at the start of the 1987/88 season. As the Wembley showpiece event of the Football
League's centenary celebrations, a Football League
side was chosen by Robson to meet a Rest of the
World XI selected by Terry Venables.

I was honoured to be chosen in the League squad,
captained by Bryan Robson, and it comprised nine

English players, three Scots, one from Wales, two from Northern Ireland, and three from the Republic – Paul McGrath, Liam Brady and me.

The World squad was full of big names including Russian goalkeeper Rinat Dasaev, Josimar from Brazil, Thomas Berthold of West Germany, France's Michel Platini and, biggest of all, Diego Maradona of Argentina, who only a year earlier had wrecked England's World Cup hopes in the 'Hand Of God' match.

To have the chance of playing against players of that pedigree was an exciting prospect. A week before that game I had played at Wembley with Everton who, as champions, met FA Cup winners Coventry in the FA Charity Shield.

But in the first half of that match, which we won 1-0 through a Wayne Clarke goal, my Achilles went – and with it my chance of coming face to face at Wembley with Maradona, Platini and company. For the record, the League side won 3-0 with two goals from Bryan Robson and one from Norman Whiteside.

Although I missed out on playing against Maradona I did once manage to have a close-up view of the great man doing free-kick target practice against a goalkeeper who might as well not have been there, for all the chance he had of stopping any of the shots!

The Greatest

It was November 1992 and I was with the Republic of Ireland squad who were due to be playing Spain in a World Cup qualifier in Seville, the club that Maradona was then playing for.

We had just finished a morning session at Seville's training ground on the morning of the match and we were about to head back to the hotel when Maradona walked onto the field with a 6ft 5ins goalkeeper and proceeded to ping shots into each top corner of the net – the giant in goal never getting anywhere near them.

So I at least have the memory of being on the same pitch as Diego, even if it was as an enthralled spectator!

Some football fans in their mid-20s and younger have only known the Premier League but the game was alive and kicking long before August, 1992. I know, because I have some stirring experiences from my career in the former top flight, the old First Division.

While there is no doubt that the Premier League era has transformed English football – the coincidental rise of satellite television making it a lucrative, global brand and the influx of foreigners giving the game an exotic flavour – there is a regrettable tendency to forget about the century of football that preceded it.

Kevin Sheedy

When I reflect on the great players I played with and against there is no doubt that many of them would star in today's game, especially with the tighter disciplinary regulations and the vastly superior quality of pitches.

I have talked in depth in other chapters about my two boyhood heroes, George Best and Bobby Charlton, as well as the best striker I played with (Adrian Heath at Everton) and the best player overall I teamed up with, that great Goodison captain and stylish, inspirational defender, Kevin Ratcliffe. But my memory bank is full of other wonderful players, colleagues and opponents, during the peak of my career with Everton and Ireland in the 1980s.

Even during my frustrating four years at Liverpool, during which I made only five first- team appearances, I played and trained with the likes of Kenny Dalglish and Graeme Souness, fantastic players in very different ways. Observing their good habits was a great learning curve for me. I was impressed by the type of training at Liverpool, nothing special but built around five-a-sides, the simple pass and move philosophy that had been introduced by Bill Shankly and continued by Bob Paisley and his staff.

Top players don't need coaching and I don't remember any coaching sessions at Liverpool. It was similar when I moved to Everton because Howard Kendall's philosophy was very like Liverpool's, with everything done with the ball and a concentration on possession. So in that sense it was a seamless transition for me.

Kenny was a world-class player who, like George Best with Northern Ireland, would have earned even greater global acclaim if he'd played with a bigger national side than Scotland. In saying that, I mean no disrespect to Kenny's deep patriotic commitment to his country.

Graeme, too, was one of the finest midfielder talents of his generation: a physical, powerful player with a delicate touch and great passing ability, wonderfully described by sportswriter David Miller as a 'bear of a man with the touch of a violinist'.

During my time at Liverpool I remember Graeme trying to close me down during a training session – so I nutmegged him, went round the other side and carried on with the ball. Graeme just laughed. Years later we were facing each other in the Milk Cup Final between Everton and Liverpool and again he came in to close me down and again I nutmegged him. But this time he didn't laugh. He stuck his elbow across my nose. That's the sort of thing he would do. He was hard but he was still a great player.

Kevin Sheedy

The classic example of an all-round box-to-box midfielder was Bryan Robson at Manchester United. He was probably the prototype. He was brave, scored goals, defended his own box when he had to but would be up in attack the next moment. He would be invaluable today.

When we played Tottenham I came up against a very different kind of midfielder in Glenn Hoddle. Some people labelled him a luxury player but he was a gifted performer with precise passing ability.

Given that the period from 1984 to the end of the decade was the most successful period in Everton history, it's not surprising that there were a host of fine players at Goodison. I would choose Neville Southall, in his pomp probably the best goalkeeper in the world, as the greatest professional during my time at Everton. You had to be good to put a shot past him in training. You had to stick the ball into one of the corners of the net to have any chance of beating him and if you ever chipped the ball over him you'd better look out!

He hated being beaten in training as much as he did in matches. They say goalkeepers are mad and Nev was right up there with them! Our goalkeeping coach and former Ireland keeper, Alan Kelly, used to throw a medicine ball into Nev's stomach to toughen his muscles and he had 'no hands' stints in training, when he would make saves just with his body.

We'd have a chance of scoring in training against our other keepers, such as Jason Kearton and Gerry Peyton, but when Nev went between the posts opportunities were few and far between. He demanded so much of himself and of his team-mates. He never settled for second best. In games where he had little to do his concentration level never dipped and he'd be switched on to make that one often crucial save.

I was at Liverpool with Ray Clemence and then Bruce Grobbelaar. Both were top keepers, worth a lot of points to the club over a season. But Nev was the best goalkeeper I've played with. For a man with such a big frame he was so agile with terrific reach. He presented a formidable barrier to the opposition.

In front of Neville, the defence that Howard built, which provided such a formidable foundation for the double of league and European Cup Winners' Cup in 1985, also took some beating. Both full-backs, Gary Stevens and Pat Van Den Hauwe – who succeeded our 1984 FA Cup-winning left-back John Bailey – were great tacklers who had pace and could also get forward, while alongside 'king' Kevin Ratcliffe at centre-back was Derek Mountfield, who scored the remarkable tally of 14 goals in 1984/85 without the aid of penalties.

I had a similar telepathic-like understanding with Derek as I had with Adrian Heath. A few of his goals came from my free-kicks and when you're about to take one you always look for someone to make a run. Derek was often first on the move and I'd try to put the ball on his head. That's how he scored the winner in the 1985 FA Cup semi-final.

Later, Dave Watson arrived to replace Derek at the heart of the Everton defence and established himself as a great defender, later succeeding Kevin as captain and coming out with that great quote when he lifted the FA Cup after beating Manchester United in 1995: "Following Kevin Ratcliffe as captain has been like walking out on stage after Frank Sinatra."

The Everton midfield I played in, with Trevor Steven on the right and Paul Bracewell and Peter Reid central, was the perfect blend. Supporters of a certain age look back fondly to the Ball-Harvey-Kendall midfield that was the heartbeat of the 1969/70 title-winning side. But I reckon our midfield of the mid-1980s will also be remembered as a wonderfully balanced combination.

As well as the previously mentioned Adrian Heath I

played with some terrific forwards at Everton. Graeme Sharp followed in the illustrious tradition of Everton centre-forwards and led the line superbly. When you think that only the fabled Dixie Dean scored more Everton goals than Graeme's 159 – and it's 160 if you add his header in the 1986 FA Cup quarter-final at Luton Town, wrongly recorded as a Mal Donaghy own goal – it speaks volumes for Graeme's quality.

During Graeme's 11 years at Everton he had an astonishing 17 different attack partners, ranging from Bob Latchford to Tony Cottee. Two I'd pick out are Andy Gray and Gary Lineker, neither of whom spent long at Goodison but who both made a significant impact.

Andy arrived in 1983 and was a massive influence both on the pitch and in the dressing room. He had a talismanic, inspirational affect on the club, which saw us go on a great post-Christmas run helping us climb the league and lift the FA Cup at Wembley.

Gary spent just the one season of 1985/86 at Goodison but scored the remarkable total of 40 goals, 30 of them in the league, but sadly we twice just missed out on silverware, finishing double runners-up to Liverpool in league and FA Cup. His goals tally was really down to the fact that we were playing more of a long-ball game, aiming to find Gary up front, so the rest of us had far fewer scoring opportunities. After Gary and Graeme Sharp (who scored 20 in league and FA Cup), the only other player in double figures was Adrian Heath with 12.

For Ireland, Paul McGrath stands out as a great performer either in midfield or at the heart of defence. Much was written about his off-field lifestyle with Manchester United and Aston Villa, but few players could have coupled that with consistently outstanding displays at both club and international level.

During my international career perhaps the only world-class player Ireland had was Liam Brady, who I've already discussed. Liam was gifted but he wasn't right for Jack Charlton's team ethic, which was collective rather than individual. Jack knew the blend he wanted and he got it from very good professionals such as Denis Irwin, Steve Staunton, Chris Hughton, Kevin Moran, Mick McCarthy, Ray Houghton and John Aldridge. No superstars, but an effective squad bonded with a fine team spirit.

John Aldridge was a proven goalscorer but I think he got frustrated playing for Ireland because Jack played with only one striker and he didn't get as many chances as he'd have liked. It meant the lone attacker, whether it was Aldo, Frank Stapleton or Tony Cas-carino, had to run himself into the ground and often had to be replaced after an hour.

The strikers certainly didn't get the best of deals in Jack's set-up in terms of scoring opportunities. It took Aldo a long time to break his duck for Ireland but, to his credit, he went on to score 19 international goals from his 69 appearances while at Oxford United, Liverpool, Real Sociedad and Tranmere Rovers.

I remember making my Ireland debut against Holland in October 1983 and came face-to-face with rising stars Ruud Gullit and Marco Van Basten. You could see they were destined for greatness and they beat us 3-2, with Gullit scoring twice and Van Basten getting Holland's other goal.

Another international opponent who made a big impression on me was Romania's Gheorghe Hagi, playmaker supreme. He did the talk – but he also did the walk. Franco Baresi of Italy was another highly impressive opponent in a playing career that has left me with wonderful memories of great team-mates and opponents.

22

Everton And Ireland
My Blues and Greens
Fantasy Football XI

AS I say, I've been privileged to play with some terrific players at club and international level so I'm going to indulge in selecting my own fantasy side drawn from team-mates at Everton and the Republic of Ireland.

It's a fascinating but far from easy task and if anyone I've played alongside feels a little bit miffed that they've not made my team I apologise. But, as they say in the game, every time you pick a team you disappoint someone. So here's my 'Blues and Greens' line-up which I've selected in a 4-4-2 formation:

GOALKEEPER:

There are two contenders for the job of last line of defence: Neville Southall and Packie Bonner. Packie was a top goalkeeper who had a great career with Celtic. His positioning was always impressive and he was a good talker with loads of experience.

But, as you might expect, I've got to go with big Nev. During our days at Everton he was the best goalkeeper in the world. I'm not the only one to have said that. He really was awesome and it's not underestimating his value to say that his saves were worth at least ten or 11 points a season to us.

Nev put in so much hard work on the training ground – he couldn't get enough of it – and thoroughly deserved the rewards he got from the game. As well as being a model professional he was also a down to earth character who, in his early Everton days, used to cycle to and from our Bellefield training ground.

RIGHT-BACK:

I'm going to pick from Chris Hughton, Denis Irwin and Gary Stevens, three tremendous players. Denis had a fine club and international career and had a great right foot. He was excellent at delivering free-kicks and he got forward well.

After starting out with Leeds United, Denis moved on to Oldham, where he must have caught the eye of Sir Alex Ferguson. He went on to tot up 368 appearances for Manchester United, where he won seven Premier League title winner's medals and a Champions League in 1999, as well as many other honours. He played for Ireland in the 1994 World Cup.

Chris was my Ireland room-mate at Italia 90 and a great lad. He, too, had an impressive club career, playing for a long time for Tottenham Hotspur before moving into coaching and management. He was good at defending and supporting attacks and his composed attitude was great for handling big games.

Gary Stevens had a terrific understanding with Trevor Steven down our right flank at Everton and both players were fine athletes. Gary was a superb defender but weighing up the trio of contenders I'm going to opt for Denis Irwin.

CENTRE-BACKS:

There's plenty of quality choice for the two players to link up at the heart of defence. From Ireland there was Kevin Moran, Mick McCarthy and Paul McGrath and at Everton Kevin Ratcliffe, Derek Mountfield and Dave Watson.

Thanks in part to his Gaelic football background, Kevin was as hard as nails. I know that from painful experience when we collided in that Everton game against Manchester United at Goodison, which I've talked about in another chapter. He was a real honest professional. He'd go in where it hurts – almost every time you saw him he'd be sporting a cut on his head – but aside from his courage he was also a really strong defender.

Mick McCarthy, as we've already discussed, was straight out of the Jack Charlton school of defending, which is why Jack picked him for Ireland. Mick was ideal for the longer ball game. He didn't have loads of pace and not many frills. But he was wholehearted and got himself in good positions for headers and tackles. He was a good leader with a powerful will to win.

I've touched on Paul McGrath's versatility, which was one of his many strengths. Paul could have played anywhere on the pitch. He was a magnificent athlete, so good he played with injuries and just shrugged them off. Whether he was operating in midfield or at the back he just cruised through games.

Paul had knee problems and I never actually saw him train. But then he didn't need to train. He'd just turn up for internationals, go out and play and probably be the best man on the pitch. He was a natural player and even without his injury problems it's hard to envisage him being any better than he was.

Turning to my Everton nominees, Derek Mountfield was a capable defender who had a great knack for scoring goals, contributing ten to our league championship success in 1984/85 and collecting another four in cups. Sadly, he had injury problems and his Everton career didn't take off as it should have done after our title year. But he left a great legacy.

Derek's successor, Dave Watson, was a typical big, strong centre-half, formidable in the tackle and powerful in the air.

As for Kevin Ratcliffe, what more needs to be said? He was a fantastic captain of Everton and Wales – that's why I devoted a complete chapter to him in this book. And he's lifted more trophies than any skipper in the club's history. That says it all. He was also the quickest footballer I ever played with, which is quite a compliment considering the number of players I knew over the course of my career.

Perhaps Gary Lineker ran him close in the speed stakes but we never saw them race each other because Gary never trained! He'd have baths and massage instead, just like Paul Bracewell.

So my choices as centre-backs are Paul McGrath on the right and Kevin Ratcliffe on the left – and Kevin would also captain my team.

LEFT-BACK:

I'm making my choice here from Pat Van Den Hauwe and John Bailey. Pat was a right-footed left-back who could get forward but who was essentially a defender. That's what he did first and foremost and he also kept me well supplied with the ball. He was also accomplished at centre-half.

John had a great left foot and was a reliable, committed defender. He was also a fantastic character. Life was never dull with Bails around. But I'm going to give my vote at left-back to Pat.

RIGHT MIDFIELD:

The contenders for this position are my Everton teammate Trevor Steven and my Republic of Ireland colleague and former Liverpool player, Ray Houghton.

Ray was a busy, lively player, always looking for the telling pass to probe the opposition defence. He would find good goalscoring positions without scoring as many goals as he would have liked to, or should have done.

He would also come inside to link up play and he was a typical Liverpool player in that he could pass the ball and keep it. Ray had great energy and could have a big influence on games.

Trevor had a bit more pace than Ray. He could go past players with ease and was a fine finisher with a great shot.

As well as being a wonderful crosser of a ball he did his stint defensively, too. So Trevor Steven just edges out Ray as my right-flank man.

CENTRE MIDFIELD:

The group from which I'll pick my central midfield pair comprise my Everton team-mates, Peter Reid and Paul Bracewell and Republic of Ireland players, Andy Townsend and Liam Brady.

Andy was a real high-energy character who could cover the whole pitch. He was a steady player who knew his role in the Ireland set-up. His performances didn't vary much. He played at a consistent level and you knew what you were going to get from him.

If Andy was the kind of bread and butter player most teams need, then Liam was totally different. He was a complete playmaker who wanted the ball all the time. He had a fantastic left foot which opened the door for him to play successfully in Italian football. He could score and create goals.

I was very tempted to choose Reidy and Brace, my Everton buddies, as the central duo. They performed so effectively together all over the pitch. Where one was, the other was, so much so we nicknamed them 'dog shites' because they got everywhere!

But Liam's considerable talents demand a place in the team so he just squeezes out Brace to line up with Reidy in the middle.

LEFT MIDFIELD:

My nominees for the left-flank spot are the Ireland trio of Ronnie Whelan, Steve Staunton and Tony Galvin and Everton's Peter Beagrie and Ian Wilson.

I got to know Ronnie early on, of course, when I was at Anfield and he went on to have a great career with Liverpool and Ireland. Tony Galvin spent the best part of a decade at Tottenham and won 29 caps for Ireland. He was also a Russian language graduate, which came in handy when we played Russia at Euro 88! Evertonians will remember Peter Beagrie – and his goal celebrations – and Ian Wilson.

But I'm going with Steve Staunton because of his all-round ability and versatility. He had a great left foot and was an impressive striker of the ball. He was also a reliable defender who was effective at set plays.

Drogheda-born Steve, who enjoyed two spells at Liverpool, is able to say that he enjoyed three World Cup experiences with Ireland. He was in Jack's team at Italia 90 and USA '94 and was called up to Mick McCarthy's squad in 2002 following the controversial departure of Roy Keane.

STRIKERS:

Contenders to be the twin strikers are John Aldridge, Frank Stapleton, Tony Cascarino, Gary Lineker, Graeme Sharp, Adrian Heath and Andy Gray.

Frank was a top striker with Arsenal and Manchester United, making more than 200 appearances for both teams. He scored 20 goals in 71 games for Ireland but wasn't really suited to the lone attacking role that Jack used. It didn't bring the best out of him.

It was similar for Tony, who wasn't the most mobile, although he put himself about and was effective at holding balls played up to him.

The system suited Aldo the best.

Early in his international career Aldo would run out of steam and become frustrated because he wasn't getting many chances. But he settled into the role and, as he got more experienced, the goals soon started to flow.

Gary Lineker proved in his one season with us at Everton in 1985/86 that he was a top class player of great pace and finishing ability. His club career also embraced three seasons at Barcelona after leaving Goodison plus a stint at Tottenham where he won an FA Cup in 1991 – not to mention 48 goals for England. That goes to prove his pedigree.

Sharpy was a terrific centre-forward for Everton, his total of 159 goals second only to Dixie Dean in the club's all-time scoring chart. But for one reason or another he never made the same impact with Scotland.

His compatriot and one of his many attack partners, Andy Gray, was like a one-man air force – fearsome with his head but fearless where he would put it! He'd have gone through a brick wall if it had been in his way, such was his courage and bravery.

As for Inchy – Adrian Heath – I've talked about him in depth elsewhere in the book and hailed him as the best striker I played with at Everton.

But for balance of blue and green up front I'm going for John Aldridge and Gary Lineker as my front two.

So here's how my team reads…I think it would give anyone a game!

Everton And Ireland

Blues & Greens XI

Neville Southall

Denis Irwin   Pat Van Den Hauwe

Paul McGrath   Kevin Ratcliffe (c)

Peter Reid   Liam Brady

Trevor Steven   Steve Staunton

John Aldridge   Gary Lineker

Substitutes: Packy Bonner, Gary Stevens, Adrian Heath, Ray Houghton, Paul Bracewell, Kevin Moran, Graeme Sharp.

Statistics & Facts
Kevin Sheedy's Professional Career
1975-1994

Compiled by John Keith & Gavin Buckland

HEREFORD UNITED

1975/76
LEAGUE:
1 appearance, 0 goals
TOTAL:
1 appearance, 0 goals

1976/77
LEAGUE:
16 appearances, 1 goal
TOTAL
16 appearances, 1 goal

1977/78
LEAGUE:
34 appearances, 3 goals

FA CUP:
2 appearances, 1 goal
LEAGUE CUP:
2 appearances + 1 sub, 0 goals
TOTAL:
38 appearances + 1 sub, 4 goals

HEREFORD UTD TOTAL:

LEAGUE:
51 appearances, 4 goals
FA CUP:
2 appearances, 1 goal
LEAGUE CUP:
2 appearances + 1 sub, 0 goals
TOTAL:
55 appearances + 1 sub, 5 goals

Statistics & Facts

LIVERPOOL

(NO APPEARANCES,
1978/79
1979/80)

1980/81
LEAGUE:
1 appearance, 0 goals
TOTAL:
1 appearance, 0 goals

1981/82
LEAGUE:
0 appearances + 2 sub, 0 goals
LEAGUE CUP:
2 appearances, 2 goals
TOTAL:
2 appearances + 2 sub, 2 goals

LIVERPOOL TOTAL:

LEAGUE:
1 appearance + 2 sub, 0 goals
LEAGUE CUP:
2 appearances, 2 goals
TOTAL:
3 appearances + 2 sub,
2 goals

EVERTON

1982/83
LEAGUE:
40 appearances, 11 goals
FA CUP:
5 appearances, 2 goals
LEAGUE CUP:
3 appearances, 0 goals
TOTAL:
48 appearances, 13 goals

1983/84
LEAGUE:
28 appearances, 4 goals
FA CUP:
6 appearances, 2 goals
LEAGUE CUP:
10 appearances, 4 goals
TOTAL:
44 appearances, 10 goals

1984/85
LEAGUE:
29 appearances, 11 goals
FA CUP:
6 appearances, 4 goals
LEAGUE CUP:
2 appearances, 0 goals
EUROPE:
5 appearances, 2 goals
TOTAL:
42 appearances, 17 goals

1985/86
LEAGUE:
31 appearances, 5 goals
FA CUP:
3 appearances, 0 goals
LEAGUE CUP:
4 appearances, 2 goals
OTHER:
5 appearances, 2 goals
TOTAL:
43 appearances, 9 goals

1986/87
LEAGUE:
28 appearances, 13 goals
FA CUP:
1 appearance, 0 goals
LEAGUE CUP:
4 appearances, 1 goal

Kevin Sheedy

OTHER:
4 appearances, 2 goals
TOTAL:
37 appearances, 16 goals

1987/88
LEAGUE:
14 appearances + 3 sub, 1 goal
LEAGUE CUP:
1 appearance, 0 goals
OTHER:
3 appearances, 0 goals
TOTAL:
18 appearances + 3 sub, 1 goal

1988/89
LEAGUE:
24 appearances + 2 sub, 8 goals
FA CUP:
8 appearances, 4 goals
LEAGUE CUP:
1 appearance + 1 sub, 0 goals
OTHER:
5 appearances, 0 goals
TOTAL:
38 appearances + 3 sub, 12 goals

1989/90
LEAGUE:
33 appearances + 4 sub, 9 goals
FA CUP:
6 appearances, 2 goals
LEAGUE CUP:
4 appearances, 2 goals
TOTAL:
43 appearances + 4 sub, 13 goals

1990/91
LEAGUE:
20 appearances + 2 sub, 4 goals
FA CUP:

3 appearances, 1 goal
OTHER:
2 appearances, 0 goals
TOTAL:
25 appearances + 2 sub, 5 goals

1991/92
LEAGUE:
16 appearances, 1 goal
LEAGUE CUP:
2 appearances, 0 goals
OTHER:
1 appearance, 0 goals
TOTAL:
19 appearances, 1 goal

EVERTON TOTAL:

LEAGUE:
263 appearances + 11 sub,
67 goals
FA CUP:
38 appearances, 15 goals
LEAGUE CUP:
31 appearances + 1 sub,
9 goals
EUROPE:
5 appearances, 2 goals
OTHER:
20 appearances, 4 goals
TOTAL:
357 appearances + 12 sub, 97
goals

NEWCASTLE UNITED

1991/92
LEAGUE:
13 appearances, 1 goal
TOTAL:
13 appearances, 1 goal

Statistics & Facts

1992/93
LEAGUE:
23 appearances + 1 sub, 3 goals
FA CUP:
2 appearances + 1 sub, 1 goal
LEAGUE CUP:
4 appearances, 0 goals
OTHER:
4 appearances, 1 goal
TOTAL:
33 appearances + 2 sub, 5 goals

NEWCASTLE UNITED TOTAL:

LEAGUE:
36 appearances + 1 sub, 4 goals
FA CUP:
2 appearances + 1 sub, 1 goal
LEAGUE CUP:
4 appearances, 0 goals
OTHER:
4 appearances, 1 goal
OVERALL:
46 appearances + 2 sub, 6 goals

BLACKPOOL

1993/94
LEAGUE:
25 appearances + 1 sub, 1 goal
LEAGUE CUP:
3 appearances, 0 goals
OTHER:
1 appearance, 0 goals
TOTAL:
29 appearances + 1 sub, 1 goal

BLACKPOOL TOTAL:

LEAGUE:
25 appearances + 1 sub, 1 goal

LEAGUE CUP:
3 appearances, 0 goals
OTHER:
1 appearance, 0 goals
OVERALL:
29 appearances + 1 sub, 1 goal

CAREER TOTAL

LEAGUE:
376 appearances + 15 sub,
76 goals

FA CUP:
42 appearances + 2 sub,
17 goals

LEAGUE CUP:
42 appearances + 2 sub, 11
goals

EUROPE:
5 appearances, 2 goals

OTHER:
25 appearances, 5 goals

OVERALL
490 appearances + 18 sub,
111 goals

* 'OTHER' INCLUDES
FA CHARITY SHIELD,
SCREEN SPORT SUPER CUP,
FULL MEMBERS CUP,
SIMOD CUP, ZENITH DATA
SYSTEMS CUP,
ANGLO-ITALIAN CUP
AND AUTOGLASS
TROPHY

Kevin Sheedy

CAREER
HONOURS

LIVERPOOL:
Four Central League medals

EVERTON:
Two League championship medals
One European Cup Winners' Cup winners medal
Three FA Cup runners-up medals
One League Cup runners-up medal
Four FA Charity Shield winners medals (includes one shared)
One Simod Cup runners-up medal
One Zenith Data Systems Cup runners-up medal
One ScreenSport Super Cup runners-up medal

NEWCASTLE UNITED:
One First Division Championship medal

FACTS & FIGURES

**His 14 goals from free-kicks
came in the following games:**

December 18, 1982: v Luton Town (First Division)
January 30, 1983: v Shrewsbury Town (FA Cup)
March 15, 1983: v Southampton (First Division)
March 9, 1985: v Ipswich Town (FA Cup)
April 13, 1985: v Luton Town (FA Cup)
April 16, 1985: v West Bromwich Albion (First Division)
November 26, 1985: v Chelsea (League Cup)
September 16, 1986 : v Liverpool (Screen Sport Super Cup)
October 11, 1986: v Charlton Athletic (First Division – 2 goals)
November 8, 1986 : v Chelsea (First Division)
April 25, 1987: v Liverpool (First Division)
May 13, 1989: v West Ham United (First Division)
March 3, 1990: v Wimbledon (First Division)

His 30 goals in cup games has been exceeded at Everton only by
Graeme Sharp (46) and Bob Latchford (32).

Statistics & Facts

In the FA Cup third-round tie at Leeds United in January 1985, he scored an unusual goal by scoring following a rebound from his own free-kick, volleying the ball home after Andy Gray had won a header when it came back off the bar – all without the ball touching the ground.

He is one of only five Everton players to have been selected for the PFA's Team of the Season on two or more occasions, doing so in 1984/85 and 1986/87.

His 97 Everton goals place him joint-10th on the all-time list of the club's scorers, and is the highest total by a non-striker. It is also the most by any Everton player without including a hat-trick.

He scored twice in a match on 11 different occasions, including two games against Manchester United. He scored more goals against Manchester United than against any other club – six in 16 appearances. He scored five times against Luton Town and five times against Wimbledon. He faced Wimbledon on four occasions in the league at their former Plough Lane ground, and scored three goals.

His two Everton goals against former club, Liverpool, both came from free-kicks at Anfield's Kop end during the 1986/87 season: in the Screen Sport Super Cup final first leg and in the old First Division.

He is believed to be one of only two Everton players to score from free-kicks twice in the same game, a feat he achieved at Charlton Athletic in the old First Division in October 1986. Leighton Baines also scored from two free-kicks in the Premier League game at West Ham United in September 2013.

He was the first Everton player to score in a nationally live televised match at Goodison, scoring an 86th-minute equaliser in the 1-1 First Division draw with Chelsea on Sunday, March 16, 1986. It was only the second headed league goal of his career, the other coming against Manchester United on October 27, 1984.

He scored from 11 of the 15 penalties he took for Everton and his four successful penalties (from four attempts) in the FA Cup stood as a club record until broken by Leighton Baines in February 2014.

Kevin Sheedy

The four penalties he failed to score from are:

10 December, 1983: v Aston Villa (home),
First Division – *wide.*

2 March, 1985: v Manchester United (away),
First Division – *saved by Gary Bailey.*

9 September, 1989: v Manchester United (home),
First Division – *saved by Jim Leighton.*

2 February, 1991: v Sunderland (home),
First Division – *saved by Tony Norman
but Sheedy scored from rebound.*

He was the first Everton player to take a penalty in a World Cup finals shoot-out. He scored against Romania at Italia 90.

His 42 Republic of Ireland caps while with Everton is a club record. He won a further four caps as a Newcastle United player. He scored nine goals in his 46 international appearances, and also played for the Republic's Youth and Under-21 teams.

He played for the Republic in all their matches at the 1988 European Championship finals in Germany, and every game in the Italia 90 World Cup finals.

His goal against England at Italia 90 was the first scored by a Republic player at a World Cup finals.

In February 2013 he was inducted into the Football Association of Ireland's Hall Of Fame at a ceremony in Dublin.

Kevin Sheedy played in three FA Cup Finals for Everton and was on the losing side on each occasion: 1985 v Manchester United 0-1; 1986 v Liverpool 1-3; 1989 v Liverpool 2-3. His Goodison team-mate Paul Bracewell had even worse fortune in FA Cup Finals, playing for Everton in the three finals above and then in the Sunderland side that lost 2-0 to Liverpool in 1992 to complete a remarkable quartet of losing appearances.

Statistics & Facts

EVERTON CAREER GAME BY GAME

Season	Date	Position	Opponent/Competition/Venue (Goals)
1982-83	28-Aug-82	11	Watford 1st Division A
1982-83	31-Aug-82	11	Aston Villa 1st Division H
1982-83	04-Sep-82	11	Tottenham Hotspur 1st Division H (1)
1982-83	08-Sep-82	11	Manchester United 1st Division A
1982-83	11-Sep-82	11	Notts County 1st Division A
1982-83	18-Sep-82	11	Norwich City 1st Division H
1982-83	25-Sep-82	11	Coventry City 1st Division A
1982-83	02-Oct-82	11	Brighton & H Albion 1st Division H
1982-83	05-Oct-82	11	Newport County League Cup A
1982-83	09-Oct-82	11	Manchester City 1st Division H
1982-83	16-Oct-82	11	Swansea City 1st Division A
1982-83	23-Oct-82	11	Sunderland 1st Division H
1982-83	27-Oct-82	11	Newport County League Cup H
1982-83	30-Oct-82	11	Southampton 1st Division A
1982-83	06-Nov-82	11	Liverpool 1st Division H
1982-83	23-Nov-82	11	Arsenal League Cup A
1982-83	27-Nov-82	11	West Ham United 1st Division A
1982-83	04-Dec-82	11	Birmingham City 1st Division H
1982-83	11-Dec-82	11	Ipswich Town 1st Division A (1)
1982-83	18-Dec-82	11	Luton Town 1st Division H (1)
1982-83	27-Dec-82	11	Stoke City 1st Division A
1982-83	28-Dec-82	11	Nottingham Forest 1st Division H
1982-83	01-Jan-83	11	West Bromwich Albion 1st Division A
1982-83	03-Jan-83	11	Tottenham Hotspur 1st Division A
1982-83	08-Jan-83	11	Newport County FA CUP A (1)
1982-83	11-Jan-83	11	Newport County FA CUP H
1982-83	15-Jan-83	11	Watford 1st Division H
1982-83	22-Jan-83	11	Norwich City 1st Division A
1982-83	30-Jan-83	11	Shrewsbury Town FA CUP H (1)
1982-83	05-Feb-83	11	Notts County 1st Division H (1)
1982-83	12-Feb-83	11	Aston Villa 1st Division A
1982-83	19-Feb-83	11	Tottenham Hotspur FA CUP H
1982-83	26-Feb-83	11	Swansea City 1st Division H
1982-83	02-Mar-83	11	Manchester City 1st Division A
1982-83	05-Mar-83	11	Sunderland 1st Division A
1982-83	12-Mar-83	11	Manchester United FA CUP A
1982-83	15-Mar-83	11	Southampton 1st Division H (1)
1982-83	19-Mar-83	11	Liverpool 1st Division A
1982-83	26-Mar-83	11	Arsenal 1st Division H
1982-83	02-Apr-83	11	Nottingham Forest 1st Division A
1982-83	04-Apr-83	11	Stoke City 1st Division H (2)
1982-83	09-Apr-83	11	Brighton & H Albion 1st Division A (2)
1982-83	19-Apr-83	11	Manchester United 1st Division H
1982-83	23-Apr-83	11	Birmingham City 1st Division A
1982-83	30-Apr-83	11	West Ham United 1st Division H
1982-83	02-May-83	11	Coventry City 1st Division H

Kevin Sheedy

Season	Date	Position	Opponent/Competition/Venue (Goals)
1982-83	07-May-83	11	Luton Town 1st Division A (2)
1982-83	14-May-83	11	Ipswich Town 1st Division H
1983-84	27-Aug-83	11	Stoke City 1st Division H
1983-84	29-Aug-83	11	West Ham United 1st Division H
1983-84	03-Sep-83	11	Coventry City 1st Division A (1)
1983-84	06-Sep-83	11	Ipswich Town 1st Division A
1983-84	10-Sep-83	11	West Bromwich Albion 1st Division H
1983-84	17-Sep-83	11	Tottenham Hotspur 1st Division A (1)
1983-84	24-Sep-83	11	Birmingham City 1st Division H
1983-84	01-Oct-83	11	Notts County 1st Division A
1983-84	04-Oct-83	11	Chesterfield League Cup A
1983-84	15-Oct-83	11	Luton Town 1st Division H
1983-84	22-Oct-83	11	Watford 1st Division H
1983-84	26-Oct-83	11	Chesterfield League Cup H
1983-84	29-Oct-83	11	Leicester City 1st Division A
1983-84	06-Nov-83	11	Liverpool 1st Division A
1983-84	09-Nov-83	11	Coventry City League Cup H
1983-84	12-Nov-83	11	Nottingham Forest 1st Division H
1983-84	19-Nov-83	11	Arsenal 1st Division A
1983-84	26-Nov-83	11	Norwich City 1st Division H
1983-84	30-Nov-83	11	West Ham United League Cup A (1)
1983-84	03-Dec-83	11	Manchester United 1st Division A (1)
1983-84	06-Dec-83	11	West Ham United League Cup H (1)
1983-84	10-Dec-83	11	Aston Villa 1st Division H
1983-84	17-Dec-83	11	Queens Park Rangers 1st Division A
1983-84	26-Dec-83	11	Sunderland 1st Division H
1983-84	27-Dec-83	11	Wolverhampton W. 1st Division A
1983-84	31-Dec-83	11	Coventry City 1st Division H
1983-84	02-Jan-84	11	Birmingham City 1st Division A
1983-84	06-Jan-84	11	Stoke City FA CUP A
1983-84	14-Jan-84	11	Stoke City 1st Division A
1983-84	18-Jan-84	11	Oxford United League Cup A
1983-84	21-Jan-84	11	Tottenham Hotspur 1st Division H
1983-84	24-Jan-84	11	Oxford United League Cup H (1)
1983-84	28-Jan-84	11	Gillingham FA CUP H
1983-84	31-Jan-84	11	Gillingham FA CUP A
1983-84	04-Feb-84	11	Notts County 1st Division H (1)
1983-84	06-Feb-84	11	Gillingham FA CUP A (2)
1983-84	11-Feb-84	11	West Bromwich Albion 1st Division A
1983-84	15-Feb-84	11	Aston Villa League Cup H (1)
1983-84	18-Feb-84	11	Shrewsbury Town FA CUP H
1983-84	22-Feb-84	11	Aston Villa League Cup A
1983-84	25-Feb-84	11	Watford 1st Division A
1983-84	03-Mar-84	11	Liverpool 1st Division H
1983-84	10-Mar-84	11	Notts County FA CUP A
1983-84	25-Mar-84	11	Liverpool League Cup N
1984-85	15-Sep-84	11	Newcastle United 1st Division A (1)

Statistics & Facts

Season	Date	Position	Opponent/Competition/Venue (Goals)
1984-85	19-Sep-84	11	UC Dublin ECW Cup A
1984-85	22-Sep-84	11	Southampton 1st Division H
1984-85	26-Sep-84	11	Sheffield United League Cup A
1984-85	29-Sep-84	11	Watford 1st Division A
1984-85	27-Oct-84	11	Manchester United 1st Division H (2)
1984-85	03-Nov-84	11	Leicester City 1st Division H (1)
1984-85	07-Nov-84	11	Inter Bratislava ECW Cup H (1)
1984-85	10-Nov-84	11	West Ham United 1st Division A
1984-85	17-Nov-84	11	Stoke City 1st Division H
1984-85	20-Nov-84	11	Grimsby Town League Cup H
1984-85	24-Nov-84	11	Norwich City 1st Division A (1)
1984-85	01-Dec-84	11	Sheffield Wednesday 1st Division H
1984-85	08-Dec-84	11	Queens Park Rangers 1st Division A
1984-85	15-Dec-84	11	Nottingham Forest 1st Division H (1)
1984-85	22-Dec-84	11	Chelsea 1st Division H
1984-85	26-Dec-84	11	Sunderland 1st Division A
1984-85	29-Dec-84	11	Ipswich Town 1st Division A
1984-85	01-Jan-85	11	Luton Town 1st Division H
1984-85	05-Jan-85	11	Leeds United FA CUP A (1)
1984-85	12-Jan-85	11	Newcastle United 1st Division H (2)
1984-85	26-Jan-85	11	Doncaster Rovers FA CUP H
1984-85	02-Feb-85	11	Watford 1st Division H (1)
1984-85	16-Feb-85	11	Telford United FA CUP H (1)
1984-85	23-Feb-85	11	Leicester City 1st Division A
1984-85	02-Mar-85	11	Manchester United 1st Division A
1984-85	06-Mar-85	11	Fortuna Sittard ECW Cup H
1984-85	09-Mar-85	11	Ipswich Town FA CUP H (1)
1984-85	03-Apr-85	11	Tottenham Hotspur 1st Division A
1984-85	06-Apr-85	11	Sunderland 1st Division H
1984-85	13-Apr-85	11	Luton Town FA CUP N (1)
1984-85	16-Apr-85	11	West Bromwich Albion 1st Division H (1)
1984-85	20-Apr-85	11	Stoke City 1st Division A (1)
1984-85	24-Apr-85	11	Bayern Munich ECW Cup H
1984-85	04-May-85	11	Sheffield Wednesday 1st Division A
1984-85	06-May-85	11	Queens Park Rangers 1st Division H
1984-85	08-May-85	11	West Ham United 1st Division H
1984-85	11-May-85	11	Nottingham Forest 1st Division A
1984-85	15-May-85	11	Rapid Vienna ECW Cup N (1)
1984-85	18-May-85	11	Manchester United FA CUP N
1984-85	23-May-85	11	Liverpool 1st Division H
1984-85	26-May-85	11	Coventry City 1st Division A
1985-86	10-Aug-85	9	Manchester United Charity Shield N
1985-86	17-Aug-85	11	Leicester City 1st Division A
1985-86	20-Aug-85	11	West Bromwich Albion 1st Division H
1985-86	24-Aug-85	11	Coventry City 1st Division H
1985-86	26-Aug-85	11	Tottenham Hotspur 1st Division A
1985-86	31-Aug-85	11	Birmingham City 1st Division H

Kevin Sheedy

Season	Date	Position	Opponent/Competition/Venue (Goals)
1985-86	03-Sep-85	11	Sheffield Wednesday 1st Division A
1985-86	14-Sep-85	11	Luton Town 1st Division H (1)
1985-86	18-Sep-85	11	Manchester United Screen Sport A (2)
1985-86	21-Sep-85	11	Liverpool 1st Division H
1985-86	25-Sep-85	11	Bournemouth League Cup H
1985-86	28-Sep-85	11	Aston Villa 1st Division A
1985-86	02-Oct-85	11	Norwich City Screen Sport H
1985-86	05-Oct-85	11	Oxford United 1st Division H
1985-86	08-Oct-85	11	Bournemouth League Cup A
1985-86	12-Oct-85	11	Chelsea 1st Division A (1)
1985-86	19-Oct-85	11	Watford 1st Division H
1985-86	23-Oct-85	11	Norwich City Screen Sport A
1985-86	26-Oct-85	11	Manchester City 1st Division A
1985-86	29-Oct-85	11	Shrewsbury Town League Cup A (1)
1985-86	02-Nov-85	11	West Ham United 1st Division A
1985-86	09-Nov-85	11	Arsenal 1st Division H
1985-86	16-Nov-85	11	Ipswich Town 1st Division A (1)
1985-86	23-Nov-85	11	Nottingham Forest 1st Division H
1985-86	26-Nov-85	11	Chelsea League Cup A (1)
1985-86	30-Nov-85	11	Southampton 1st Division A
1985-86	07-Dec-85	11	West Bromwich Albion 1st Division A (1)
1985-86	21-Dec-85	11	Coventry City 1st Division A
1985-86	26-Dec-85	11	Manchester United 1st Division H
1985-86	28-Dec-85	11	Sheffield Wednesday 1st Division H
1985-86	01-Jan-86	11	Newcastle United 1st Division A
1985-86	11-Jan-86	11	Queens Park Rangers 1st Division H
1985-86	25-Jan-86	11	Blackburn Rovers FA CUP H
1985-86	11-Feb-86	11	Manchester City 1st Division H
1985-86	12-Mar-86	11	Luton Town FA CUP H
1985-86	16-Mar-86	11	Chelsea 1st Division H (1)
1985-86	19-Mar-86	11	Tottenham Hotspur Screen Sport H
1985-86	22-Mar-86	11	Luton Town 1st Division A
1985-86	26-Apr-86	11	Nottingham Forest 1st Division A
1985-86	30-Apr-86	11	Oxford United 1st Division A
1985-86	03-May-86	11	Southampton 1st Division H
1985-86	05-May-86	11	West Ham United 1st Division H
1985-86	10-May-86	11	Liverpool FA CUP N
1986-87	16-Aug-86	11	Liverpool Charity Shield N
1986-87	23-Aug-86	11	Nottingham Forest 1st Division H (2)
1986-87	25-Aug-86	11	Sheffield Wednesday 1st Division A
1986-87	30-Aug-86	11	Coventry City 1st Division A
1986-87	02-Sep-86	11	Oxford United 1st Division H
1986-87	06-Sep-86	11	Queens Park Rangers 1st Division H
1986-87	13-Sep-86	11	Wimbledon 1st Division A (1)
1986-87	16-Sep-86	11	Liverpool Screen Sport A (1)
1986-87	21-Sep-86	11	Manchester United 1st Division H (1)
1986-87	27-Sep-86	11	Tottenham Hotspur 1st Division A

Statistics & Facts

Season	Date	Position	Opponent/Competition/Venue (Goals)
1986-87	30-Sep-86	11	Liverpool Screen Sport H
1986-87	04-Oct-86	11	Arsenal 1st Division H
1986-87	07-Oct-86	11	Newport County League Cup A
1986-87	11-Oct-86	11	Charlton Athletic 1st Division A (2)
1986-87	28-Oct-86	11	Sheffield Wednesday League Cup H
1986-87	02-Nov-86	11	West Ham United 1st Division A
1986-87	08-Nov-86	11	Chelsea 1st Division H (1)
1986-87	15-Nov-86	11	Leicester City 1st Division A (1)
1986-87	19-Nov-86	11	Norwich City League Cup A (1)
1986-87	23-Nov-86	11	Liverpool 1st Division H
1986-87	29-Nov-86	11	Manchester City 1st Division A
1986-87	03-Dec-86	11	Newcastle United Full Members Cup H (1)
1986-87	06-Dec-86	11	Norwich City 1st Division H
1986-87	13-Dec-86	11	Luton Town 1st Division A
1986-87	20-Dec-86	11	Wimbledon 1st Division H (1)
1986-87	26-Dec-86	11	Newcastle United 1st Division A
1986-87	28-Dec-86	11	Leicester City 1st Division H (1)
1986-87	01-Jan-87	11	Aston Villa 1st Division H (1)
1986-87	03-Jan-87	11	Queens Park Rangers 1st Division A
1986-87	10-Jan-87	11	Southampton FA CUP H
1986-87	17-Jan-87	11	Sheffield Wednesday 1st Division H
1986-87	21-Jan-87	11	Liverpool League Cup H
1986-87	25-Jan-87	11	Nottingham Forest 1st Division A
1986-87	04-Apr-87	11	Chelsea 1st Division A
1986-87	11-Apr-87	11	West Ham United 1st Division H
1986-87	18-Apr-87	11	Aston Villa 1st Division A (1)
1986-87	25-Apr-87	11	Liverpool 1st Division A (1)
1987-88	01-Aug-87	11	Coventry City Charity Shield N
1987-88	29-Aug-87	12	Sheffield Wednesday 1st Division H
1987-88	02-Sep-87	13	Queens Park Rangers 1st Division A
1987-88	14-Nov-87	11	West Ham United 1st Division H
1987-88	17-Nov-87	11	Oldham Athletic League Cup H
1987-88	21-Nov-87	11	Portsmouth 1st Division A
1987-88	25-Nov-87	11	Bayern Munich Lge Centenary H
1987-88	28-Nov-87	11	Oxford United 1st Division H
1987-88	05-Dec-87	11	Charlton Athletic 1st Division A
1987-88	12-Dec-87	11	Derby County 1st Division H
1987-88	19-Dec-87	11	Arsenal 1st Division A
1987-88	16-Feb-88	6	Luton Town Simod Cup H
1987-88	05-Mar-88	11	Newcastle United 1st Division H
1987-88	09-Mar-88	11	Tottenham Hotspur 1st Division A
1987-88	12-Mar-88	11	Chelsea 1st Division A
1987-88	20-Mar-88	11	Liverpool 1st Division H
1987-88	26-Mar-88	11	Watford 1st Division A (1)
1987-88	29-Mar-88	11	Wimbledon 1st Division H
1987-88	04-Apr-88	11	West Ham United 1st Division A
1987-88	09-Apr-88	11	Portsmouth 1st Division H

Kevin Sheedy

Season	Date	Position	Opponent/Competition/Venue (Goals)
1987-88	07-May-88	13	Arsenal 1st Division H
1988-89	27-Aug-88	12	Newcastle United 1st Division H
1988-89	29-Aug-88	11	Manchester United Mercantile Trophy A
1988-89	03-Sep-88	11	Coventry City 1st Division A
1988-89	10-Sep-88	11	Nottingham Forest 1st Division H
1988-89	17-Sep-88	11	Millwall 1st Division A
1988-89	24-Sep-88	11	Luton Town 1st Division H
1988-89	27-Sep-88	11	Bury League Cup H
1988-89	01-Oct-88	11	Wimbledon 1st Division A
1988-89	14-Dec-88	12	Bradford City League Cup A
1988-89	17-Dec-88	12	Queens Park Rangers 1st Division A
1988-89	20-Dec-88	11	Millwall Simod Cup H
1988-89	26-Dec-88	11	Middlesbrough 1st Division H
1988-89	31-Dec-88	11	Coventry City 1st Division H (2)
1988-89	02-Jan-89	11	Nottingham Forest 1st Division A
1988-89	07-Jan-89	11	West Bromwich Albion FA CUP A (1)
1988-89	11-Jan-89	11	West Bromwich Albion FA CUP H (1)
1988-89	14-Jan-89	11	Arsenal 1st Division H
1988-89	18-Jan-89	11	Wimbledon Simod Cup A
1988-89	21-Jan-89	11	Luton Town 1st Division A
1988-89	28-Jan-89	11	Plymouth Argyle FA CUP A (1)
1988-89	31-Jan-89	11	Plymouth Argyle FA CUP H (1)
1988-89	11-Feb-89	11	Southampton 1st Division A (1)
1988-89	14-Feb-89	11	Aston Villa 1st Division H
1988-89	18-Feb-89	11	Barnsley FA CUP A
1988-89	25-Feb-89	11	Derby County 1st Division A
1988-89	28-Feb-89	11	Queens Park Rangers Simod Cup H
1988-89	11-Mar-89	11	Sheffield Wednesday 1st Division H
1988-89	19-Mar-89	11	Wimbledon FA CUP H
1988-89	22-Mar-89	11	Newcastle United 1st Division A
1988-89	25-Mar-89	11	Millwall 1st Division H (1)
1988-89	27-Mar-89	11	Middlesbrough 1st Division A (1)
1988-89	01-Apr-89	11	Queens Park Rangers 1st Division H (1)
1988-89	08-Apr-89	11	Arsenal 1st Division A
1988-89	10-Apr-89	11	Charlton Athletic 1st Division H (1)
1988-89	15-Apr-89	11	Norwich City FA CUP N
1988-89	22-Apr-89	11	Tottenham Hotspur 1st Division A
1988-89	30-Apr-89	11	Nottingham Forest Simod Cup N
1988-89	03-May-89	11	Liverpool 1st Division H
1988-89	06-May-89	11	Norwich City 1st Division A
1988-89	13-May-89	11	West Ham United 1st Division H (1)
1988-89	20-May-89	11	Liverpool FA CUP N
1989-90	19-Aug-89	11	Coventry City 1st Division A
1989-90	22-Aug-89	11	Tottenham Hotspur 1st Division H (1)
1989-90	26-Aug-89	11	Southampton 1st Division H
1989-90	30-Aug-89	11	Sheffield Wednesday 1st Division A (1)
1989-90	09-Sep-89	11	Manchester United 1st Division H

Statistics & Facts

Season	Date	Position	Opponent/Competition/Venue (Goals)
1989-90	16-Sep-89	11	Charlton Athletic 1st Division A
1989-90	19-Sep-89	11	Leyton Orient League Cup A (1)
1989-90	23-Sep-89	11	Liverpool 1st Division H
1989-90	30-Sep-89	11	Crystal Palace 1st Division A
1989-90	03-Oct-89	11	Leyton Orient League Cup H (1)
1989-90	14-Oct-89	11	Millwall 1st Division H (1)
1989-90	21-Oct-89	11	Arsenal 1st Division H
1989-90	24-Oct-89	11	Luton Town League Cup H
1989-90	28-Oct-89	11	Norwich City 1st Division A
1989-90	05-Nov-89	11	Aston Villa 1st Division A
1989-90	11-Nov-89	11	Chelsea 1st Division H
1989-90	18-Nov-89	11	Wimbledon 1st Division H (1)
1989-90	22-Nov-89	11	Nottingham Forest League Cup A
1989-90	25-Nov-89	11	Nottingham Forest 1st Division A
1989-90	02-Dec-89	11	Coventry City 1st Division H
1989-90	09-Dec-89	11	Tottenham Hotspur 1st Division A
1989-90	17-Dec-89	11	Manchester City 1st Division H
1989-90	26-Dec-89	11	Derby County 1st Division A
1989-90	30-Dec-89	11	Queens Park Rangers 1st Division A
1989-90	10-Jan-90	11	Middlesbrough FA CUP H (1)
1989-90	13-Jan-90	11	Southampton 1st Division A
1989-90	17-Jan-90	11	Middlesbrough FA CUP H
1989-90	20-Jan-90	11	Sheffield Wednesday 1st Division H (2)
1989-90	28-Jan-90	11	Sheffield Wednesday FA CUP A
1989-90	03-Feb-90	11	Liverpool 1st Division A
1989-90	10-Feb-90	11	Charlton Athletic 1st Division H
1989-90	17-Feb-90	11	Oldham Athletic FA CUP A
1989-90	21-Feb-90	11	Oldham Athletic FA CUP H (1)
1989-90	03-Mar-90	11	Wimbledon 1st Division A (1)
1989-90	10-Mar-90	11	Oldham Athletic FA CUP A
1989-90	14-Mar-90	11	Manchester United 1st Division A
1989-90	17-Mar-90	11	Crystal Palace 1st Division H
1989-90	21-Mar-90	11	Millwall 1st Division A
1989-90	24-Mar-90	11	Norwich City 1st Division H
1989-90	31-Mar-90	11	Arsenal 1st Division A
1989-90	04-Apr-90	12	Nottingham Forest 1st Division H
1989-90	07-Apr-90	12	Queens Park Rangers 1st Division H
1989-90	14-Apr-90	6	Luton Town 1st Division A
1989-90	16-Apr-90	12	Derby County 1st Division H (1)
1989-90	21-Apr-90	11	Manchester City 1st Division A
1989-90	28-Apr-90	11	Chelsea 1st Division A
1989-90	05-May-90	12	Aston Villa 1st Division H (1)
1990-91	25-Aug-90	12	Leeds United 1st Division H
1990-91	01-Sep-90	11	Manchester City 1st Division A
1990-91	10-Nov-90	10	Sheffield United 1st Division A
1990-91	18-Nov-90	11	Tottenham Hotspur 1st Division H
1990-91	24-Nov-90	11	Wimbledon 1st Division A (1)

Kevin Sheedy

Season	Date	Position	Opponent/Competition/Venue (Goals)
1990-91	01-Dec-90	11	Manchester United 1st Division H
1990-91	08-Dec-90	11	Coventry City 1st Division H
1990-91	26-Dec-90	10	Aston Villa 1st Division H
1990-91	29-Dec-90	10	Derby County 1st Division H
1990-91	01-Jan-91	10	Chelsea 1st Division A
1990-91	05-Jan-91	10	Charlton Athletic FA CUP A
1990-91	13-Jan-91	10	Manchester City 1st Division H (1)
1990-91	19-Jan-91	10	Arsenal 1st Division A
1990-91	22-Jan-91	10	Sunderland Zenith Data Cup H
1990-91	27-Jan-91	10	Woking FA CUP H (1)
1990-91	02-Feb-91	10	Sunderland 1st Division H (1)
1990-91	09-Feb-91	10	Liverpool 1st Division A
1990-91	17-Feb-91	10	Liverpool FA CUP A
1990-91	23-Mar-91	8	Nottingham Forest 1st Division H
1990-91	30-Mar-91	11	Aston Villa 1st Division A
1990-91	01-Apr-91	11	Norwich City 1st Division H
1990-91	07-Apr-91	11	Crystal Palace Zenith Data Cup N
1990-91	13-Apr-91	11	Chelsea 1st Division H
1990-91	20-Apr-91	11	Crystal Palace 1st Division A
1990-91	24-Apr-91	12	Tottenham Hotspur 1st Division A
1990-91	08-May-91	6	Derby County 1st Division A (1)
1990-91	11-May-91	6	Queens Park Rangers 1st Division A
1991-92	17-Aug-91	8	Nottingham Forest 1st Division A
1991-92	20-Aug-91	8	Arsenal 1st Division H
1991-92	24-Aug-91	8	Manchester United 1st Division H
1991-92	28-Aug-91	8	Sheffield Wednesday 1st Division A
1991-92	31-Aug-91	11	Liverpool 1st Division A
1991-92	03-Sep-91	10	Norwich City 1st Division H
1991-92	07-Sep-91	10	Crystal Palace 1st Division H
1991-92	14-Sep-91	10	Sheffield United 1st Division A
1991-92	17-Sep-91	10	Manchester City 1st Division A
1991-92	21-Sep-91	10	Coventry City 1st Division H
1991-92	24-Sep-91	10	Watford League Cup H
1991-92	28-Sep-91	10	Chelsea 1st Division A
1991-92	01-Oct-91	11	Oldham Athletic Zenith Data Cup H
1991-92	05-Oct-91	10	Tottenham Hotspur 1st Division H
1991-92	08-Oct-91	10	Watford League Cup A
1991-92	19-Oct-91	11	Aston Villa 1st Division H
1991-92	26-Oct-91	10	Queens Park Rangers 1st Division A
1991-92	14-Dec-91	10	Oldham Athletic 1st Division A (1)
1991-92	21-Dec-91	10	Arsenal 1st Division A